Make way

– Public Praise –

Handbook & Street Songs from:

SHINE, JESUS, SHINE

A CARNIVAL OF PRAISE

THE GIFT and THE CROSS

Graham Kendrick

MAKE WAY MUSIC

KINGSWAY MUSIC
EASTBOURNE

This edition published 1991

United Kingdom:
Christian Music Association
Glyndley Manor
Stone Cross
Pevensey
East Sussex BN24 5BS

United States:
CCL Inc
7031 NE Halsey
Portland
OR-97213-6359

ISBN 0 86065 934 8

Use of Lyrics Sections

The lyrics which appear on pages 75–81, 100–104, 158–163 and 203–208 have been designed for use in public presentations. The publishers give permission for these pages only to be reproduced without charge, provided that your church or organisation holds a current Church Copyright Licence issued by the Christian Music Association. The normal terms and conditions of the licence will apply.

Full details of the Copyright Licence are available from the Christian Music Association, Glyndley Manor, Stone Cross, Pevensey, East Sussex BN24 5BS.

Thankyou Music Publishing
is administered in Europe by Thankyou Music, PO Box 75, Eastbourne
BN23 6NW, UK

Printed in Great Britain for
KINGSWAY MUSIC LTD
1 St Anne's Road, Eastbourne, E. Sussex BN21 3UN by
Stanley L. Hunt (Printers) Ltd., Rushden, Northants.

SUMMARY OF CONTENTS

The full Contents of each section is listed at the beginning of each 'Make Way'.

ACKNOWLEDGEMENTS

Compiled by Hilary Brand, Tim Morgan and Mark Kensington with assistance from Peter Brand, Mike Burn, Rose Kelbert, Jill Kendrick, Dave Liggins, Diana McKinnon Jacky Males, Stephanie Marriot, Sue Mitchell, Mike Oakes, Mary Packer, Geoff Shearn, Jo Thomas and Graham Warner.

Designed by Ron Bryant-Funnell.

Cartoons in the Streetwise Evangelism Section are based on original artwork by John Pickering from *One to One* copyright Scripture Union, and those on pages 12, 24, 32, 33, 76–81, 100–104, 115, 117, 119, 121–123 are by Sam Thompson.

The Make Way Handbook

Shine, Jesus, Shine
and
A carnival of praise

CONTENTS

MAKE WAY FOR JESUS

MAKE WAY FOR THE KING

INTRODUCTION

In 1869 a Salvation Army reporter wrote in their paper T*he East London Evangelist*:

'We have been much blessed in missioning the streets where the poorest reside. As we go singing down the street . . . doors fly open and windows shoot up, and soon we have eyes and ears on us from all sides. Every now and then we . . . pause, sing a verse or two, give a short address, publishing the glorious gospel . . . offer a few short earnest prayers; and then go on to another corner . . . .'

Praise, prayer and witness processions are by no means a new phenomenon! Outdoor events have had a special place in many phases of the church's history, and I believe that we are entering such a phase today.

Prayer, praise and witness processions can achieve many goals, from spiritual warfare to a joyful public witness to an expression of Christian unity. There is a dynamic involved which could be a key to a great spiritual breakthrough for the church, if only we could grasp it and use it. That dynamic is the strong, public declaration and celebration of truth. Satan's kingdom is built upon his lies and deceptions, but the truth that Jesus declared, when proclaimed with faith, is the very power that sets free those blinded by untruth. That power is greatly strengthened when spoken by throngs of people in unison.

Jesus said that the words He spoke were spirit and life. He has given us His words, and they can be spirit and life in our mouths, too. How desperately we need to rediscover that the truths we believe are not just concepts to hold in our minds. They are to be imbued by faith and the power of the Holy Spirit and so become divinely powered weapons in our spiritual warfare. It makes little difference whether they are spoken or sung. Every believer needs to learn how to use the 'sword of the Spirit'. We need to sing and celebrate with joyful authority the truth that Jesus Christ is the Son of God, born of a virgin, crucified, dead, buried, but raised to life. We need to proclaim that He is reigning at the right hand of the Father, soon to return to judge this world. We need to be a holy church, declaring with one voice these and other truths and living them out in the power of the Holy Spirit. As such we would be an unstoppable force.

I hope that the music and text of these processions will provide a useful tool for a prophetic church as it seeks to make the King of kings known to the ends of the earth in this generation.

MAKE WAY – WHY PRAISE PROCESSIONS?

With some notable exceptions, the streets of our villages, towns and cities have on the whole been left alone by the church, and the unpopular jobs of prayer and evangelism in the open air left to small, specialist groups with above-average boldness and below- average support from the rest of us. This state of affairs is nothing new as is clear when we look at the history of such movements as the early Methodists, or the Salvation Army (see page 20). It is, of course, easy to see how much more attractive it is to worship, pray or evangelise in the comfort and safety of a building, surrounded by a majority of sympathetic believers, rather than out in a public place surrounded by a majority of indifferent, curious or even antagonistic unbelievers.

However, a church that is too apathetic and afraid to risk the relatively minor inconveniences of such activities is never going to turn the tide of unbelief and evil in a locality, let alone reach the whole world for Christ – something which we are told is possible in one generation. For too long we have abdicated responsibility for the public, visible declaration of our faith, and abandoned the streets to political marches, political activists, cults, charity collectors, carnivals, and in many places to seedy street- life and an epidemic of violence. Political activity and carnivals can be entirely legitimate, but we believe it is time once again to invade the streets in the name of Christ!

VISIBILITY

Much has happened over the past twenty years in terms of church renewal, and many churches have sprung up, both within and without traditional denominations, full of new life and fresh expressions of God's presence among them. But this movement has been very much of an underground stream, and the general public has been largely unaware of what an attractive place 'church' can be. On more than one occasion, I have heard people who have seen Christians joyfully praising God comment: 'If I thought church was like that, I'd seriously think about going.'

It is time for the whole nation to recognise that the Christian church is a major force to be reckoned with, that it has a prophetic voice and a vital message to put across. Recent events show that Christians are keen to gather in very large numbers in a joyful, peaceful and responsible way.

But there is much more to this whole vision than a show of strength. After all, the Lord said that it is 'not by might, nor by power, but by My Spirit' (Zech 4:6) that victories are won. The kind of strength in which we must stand as Christians, and the weapons God has given us – His word, prayer, the blood of Jesus, and our testimony to Him – are foolish in the world's view. Yet God has chosen the foolish things of this world to confound the so-called wise, and the weak things of this world to confound the strong (1 Cor 1:27, 28). Therefore we can march out with courage and gladness, praying and praising, declaring the truth of

God's word, and bearing testimony to Jesus who in the apparent weakness and foolishness of crucifixion won the decisive battle against the powers of sin and death and all their terrible consequences.

SPIRITUAL DYNAMICS

What are the particular 'dynamics' which make praise, prayer and witness processions effective?

Jesus described His words in this way: 'The words I have spoken to you are spirit and they are life' (Jn 6:63). Because the source of Jesus' words was in God himself, they were not only the truth in content, but were also endorsed by the accompanying activity of the Holy Spirit. As Jesus preached the good news of the kingdom of God, His words were authenticated by the signs and wonders that followed – He spoke and diseased bodies were healed, He spoke prophetically and shaped the future. His words were the breath of God, creating or destroying by the power of the Holy Spirit. The amazing fact is that God has given *us* His words, and His Spirit! All of us have the potential to speak and sing 'Spirit-energised words' – timeless Scripture impacting today's world with the same prophetic power as it did in Jesus' day.

DECLARATION – PROCLAMATION

For many Christians, the songs they sing are just pleasant anthems, pieces of cultural heritage, or poetic theology to be preserved. A new song is sometimes valued only for its novelty, or a hymn used merely as a programme-filler in a meeting. If this is our view, then that may be all they amount to in practice. My conviction is that properly understood and rightly used, our songs can become the spiritual equivalent of rockets exploding with joy in heaven and wreaking havoc in hell! How? Because our songs contain the most powerful energy in the universe – the word of God. In the deliberate act of singing praise, we lift the word of God up before heaven, before hell, and before men and women – and God does the rest.

'. . . our songs can become . . . rockets exploding with joy in heaven and wreaking havoc in hell!'

This is one of the strongest dynamics of street marches, simply because the word of God is the Holy Spirit's sword, and when His people take His word by faith and declare it in the power of the Holy Spirit, God acts to confirm and carry out His word. We make a vital connection between God's word and every day reality when we declare, for example, that God is a just God when passing a building which symbolises something to do with justice or injustice, than when shut away in a cosy church lounge.

We learn more about this dynamic from 2 Corinthians 10 which describes the nature of spiritual strongholds. According to this passage, the power of evil in the world is channelled through false ideas, 'arguments' and 'pretensions' that set themselves up against the knowledge of God. Any Christian who has stood against Godless ideologies knows that they are more than just ideas; they carry enormous spiritual power and hold people in their grip. Jesus came into this deceived world and declared: 'You will know the truth, and the truth will set you free' (Jn 8:32). The truth needs to be declared with authority, with love and humility, and with joy. When this happens the power of God's word, which would otherwise remain hidden, is released as the supremely potent force.

Once we have discovered that spiritual power is released when we praise in this way, we must take care that we avoid a subtle danger. Our focus can easily shift from the Lord Himself, and our delight in Him, to our spiritual enemies. I believe that the effect of praise on the powers of evil must be regarded as secondary, our primary aim being to praise God for who He is. When King Jehoshaphat sent the singers out in front of the army (2 Chron 20) they were appointed 'to sing to the Lord and to praise Him for the splendour of his holiness . . . saying: "Give thanks to the Lord, for His love endures for ever." ' Theirs was a joyful song, pre-occupied with God. As they praised Him, He dealt with their enemies.

CONFESSION AND INTERCESSION

It is the privilege and responsibility of the church to stand before God on behalf of the nation in which it is placed, and to pray. Daniel is a prime example of someone who not only prayed for his own nation, as well as the one in which he was an exile, but also confessed their sins before the Lord even though he himself was a righteous man. Make Way events provide a framework in which this can be done. They can take confession and intercession to places where the need for God's mercy and forgiveness is most apparent, and where the consequences of sin are hurting people the most.

It is tremendously important that we as the church confess our part in failing to speak out and act in our society as we should have done. Confession militates against the appearance of condemning others in a self-righteous way. Confession should progress into intercession as we seek to catch what is on God's heart for the nation, city, town or village, and set our eyes on the future.

WARNING

A look at Ezekiel 33 suggests that those who claim to speak from God have a grave responsibility to warn of the consequences of rebellion against God's laws of love, as well as to proclaim the good news. Again, we have no right to be judgemental or superior, rather we should speak out of humility and compassion.

THE WITNESS OF OUR PRESENCE

It is not only the words we speak that witness to Christ, but also our very presence, and what people read in our faces, behaviour and attitudes. In addition, we should not underestimate the impact made on people as they sense God's presence with us as we pass. Let us not forget that genuine joy, love, hope and friendliness are in short supply on the streets, and for some people merely to sense the atmosphere is enough to convince them that God is real and among us. Of course, we must not think that we can switch on the Holy Spirit at our convenience. Rather, Scripture shows that it is often in worship that God chooses to manifest His presence in a special way. Once again, our part is to praise, pray and witness. He does the rest. Our joyful and colourful presence on the streets also serves to break the caricatures of Christianity that exist in people's minds, and reintroduce them to the church as a joyful company of people, full of life and colour, with a message relevant to today's world. (A march is an excellent springboard for all kinds of ancillary evangelistic activities, and some ideas are presented later in this handbook.)

It is important to keep firmly in mind that we witness not only to people, but also to spiritual powers that influence our society. On the positive side, we worship and proclaim with 'the whole company of heaven', who are constantly singing God's praise and declaring His attributes, but we also confront the powers of darkness with the truth of Christ. Paul describes his own part in this calling of the church in Ephesians 3:9-10 – 'to make all men see what is the plan of the mystery hidden for ages in God who created all things; that through the church the manifold wisdom of God might now be made known to the principalities and powers in the heavenly places' (Revised Standard Version).

MARCHING IN UNITY

The phenomenon of churches from different traditions, denominations and locations marching, witnessing and praying together is a very dynamic one. 'When brothers live together in unity . . . there the Lord bestows his blessing,' wrote the Psalmist (Ps 133:1,3). Just how much the work of God's Spirit is restricted by disunity hardly bears thinking about, and sheer ignorance of the life of other Christian groups leaves a vacuum of friendship, love and co-operation. However, when we can gather together under the banner of Christ and celebrate the basic truths of the gospel, who knows what fresh moves of the Spirit there might be, and what sharing of resources and opportunities to love and serve might occur?

There is also the 'dynamic' of agreeing together over an issue as the Spirit moves a great crowd to pray together. Let's push the limits of what can be achieved by such praying until we discover in practice that there are no limits.

A BAPTISM OF BOLDNESS

If there was no other benefit to praise, prayer and witness processions than an increasing boldness on behalf of the participants, then I feel the whole event would still be very worthwhile. I frequently wonder at the difference in atmosphere among a group of marchers before and after a march. Before, they are often reserved and restrained, nervous if they have never done anything like it before, possibly feeling foolish holding a banner, or fearful of having to pass out leaflets to strangers (or friends!). After . . . every march that I have personally seen has ended with a great sense of excitement, with many individuals set free in their spirits through the act of public confession of their faith. Many will have witnessed to their belief 'en masse' or one to one for the first time, and exchanged their shyness for boldness. Make sure that this boldness and enthusiasm is harnessed immediately (see pages 47–48, the section 'Beware the Fizzle Factor!', and further ideas for street events).

Can we measure the concrete effects of such declarations, or are we merely fooling ourselves about their power and effects? It is hard to quantify the results of such activities immediately. Essentially they are an act of faith, but if that faith is genuine then it will bear fruit in time. There have been exciting reports of people being converted during marches, and reports of an unusual openness to the Gospel on the streets and in town centres immediately following or during a march. I believe that this will increase.

But this is not primarily the aim. Where serious prayer, praise and witness marches take place as part of an on-going programme (including practical action for justice and for people in need), we aim for breakthrough in some of the following areas:

(1) A new openness to the Gospel; fresh opportunities to witness resulting in more conversions.
(2) The exposure of corruption and the breaking of evil and unjust practices in areas of society.
(3) Positive change in the policies, practices or laws of governing bodies.
(4) The establishment of more God-fearing people in places of responsibility.
(5) Breakthroughs in establishing new churches in the areas where the march takes place.
(6) Greater unity and co-operation between churches and Christian organisations.
(7) A greater awareness of the local church's message and character by the surrounding community.
(8) A new spirit of boldness among participating Christians.

NB: We may also encounter increasing opposition from some quarters.

The above are all potential areas for breakthrough. I do not wish to set any limits on what is possible, for our God specialises in impossibilities. However, praise and witness marches involve spiritual warfare, and there is a danger that people will adopt unrealistic aims in dealing with the powers of darkness, especially if seen as a one-off event. I am more and more convinced that the message of Exodus 23:30 is appropriate in this respect: 'Little by little I will drive them out before you, until you have increased enough to take possession of the land.' If we really want to break the grip of the powers of darkness in a locality, it may need to happen little by little as the church grows in authority, love and holiness.

Furthermore, it is unhelpful if unbelievers are subjected to singing, praising and shouting Christians who they know very well never do anything practical to bring righteousness and justice into the locality. Such events ideally go alongside involvement in the needs of the whole person so that we are not seen simply as people full of hot air, without real substance in our lives.

A FLEXIBLE RESOURCE

Many different ingredients go to make up a praise, prayer and witness procession. Although all the *Make Way* marches are fixed sequences, in practice the strength and emphasis of the various ingredients can be altered to fine-tune the content as required in each situation. Prayer of one kind or another may particularly need to be organised, or perhaps strong praise, witness, or an expression of unity. Corporate prayers, shouts, etc, can be added as appropriate, additional prayer scripts relating to the march route appended in a programme, and the visual appearance of the march adapted as required. For example, a march for the sole purpose of prayer may not necessarily need to go through a busy shopping street, or give as much attention to visual effects (though banners carried with faith can be as much a declaration to the spiritual powers as words spoken or sung).

'NOW IS THE TIME FOR US TO MARCH UPON THE LAND'

It seems to me and many others that now is a crucial time to invade the streets with the above aims in view. We often forget that we are among a privileged minority of nations that are freely able to undertake this kind of public demonstration. Even in Britain tighter restrictions have recently been placed on marches, and there are many powerful groups who would like to see Christians effectively banned from streets altogether. We need to make the most of the present opportunity and establish a strong presence among all the other groups who regularly demonstrate, celebrate or 'evangelise' on the streets. However, of far greater importance than 'staking our claim' in this area of the nation's life is the ever-present urgency of taking the good news of the kingdom of God to the people, through prayer, through praise and proclamation, and through witness and practical action.

To me, what is most exciting is not just filling the streets with processions, but what the whole initiative might lead to once Christians have gained a new confidence and boldness in the public arena of their community, and indeed their nation.

NOTHING NEW – SOME GLIMPSES OF CHURCH HISTORY

'There is nothing new under the sun,' as the world-weary writer of Ecclesiastes commented (Eccles 1:9). Worship in the open air is no exception – it has all been done before. The interesting thing is that where it has been done before it has very often been connected with religious revival.

The earliest record in England of Christian songs being used outdoors is in AD 675. Alfred the Great's handbook records how Aldhelm, the Abbott of Malmesbury, decided that if the people wouldn't come to the message then the message would have to come to them. Aldhelm had studied music in Rome. When he returned to Wessex, the people obviously liked his music, but had taken to leaving church before the sermon started. As they came out, Aldhelm would be there singing the popular songs of the day, progressing to songs with a Christian message and slipping in a crafty preach when he'd gathered a crowd!

The medieval monks were the evangelists of their day and many of them didn't hesitate to use new forms of music in their missions. St Bernard of Clairvaux (1090-1153) founded his own monastery and was a great church reformer, but he also moved among the common people, preaching, singing and performing signs and wonders in the open fields and town squares. Maybe this timeless hymn was first made popular among peasants in the French counryside:

> Jesus, Thou joy of loving hearts,
> Thou fount of life, Thou light of men,
> From the best bliss which earth imparts,
> We turn unfilled to Thee again.

John Huss, leader of a revival movement in the fifteenth century, composed folk hymns in his native Czech for his followers to sing as they met in market-places, fields and meadows.

The Catholic and Orthodox churches still continue the tradition of processions in many places today, particularly those associated with pilgrimage. The banners you often see hanging inside Anglican churches were not intended for that purpose, but for taking out around the parish. Whit Sunday has always been a time for Christian processions, especially in the Midlands and the North of England.

The idea of taking the Gospel out to where the people are hasn't always met with enthusiasm, even among church leaders. John Wesley was shocked when it was first suggested that he might preach to the miners of Bristol out in the fields:

'31st March 1739 . . . I thought the saving of souls almost a sin if it had not been done in a church.'

He pondered the problem and reflected that Jesus did most of his preaching outdoors:

'2nd April 1739 . . . At 4 in the afternoon I submitted to be more vile and proclaimed in the highways the glad tidings of salvation.'

It is interesting to speculate what might have happened to the history of the church, and even of our nation, if Wesley had not 'submitted to be more vile.'

The Salvation Army took their brass bands onto the streets in the late nineteenth century. They were not always very popular. *The Worthing Gazette* of 1883 described them as 'excitable young men and hysterical young women who mistake a quasi-religious revelry for Godliness.' At about the same time *Punch* magazine wrote about 'Bootheration':

> A procession is a nuisance at any time, and should only be permitted on rare and exceptional occasions. As to the noisy Religious Services which disturb the peace and quiet of neighbourhoods on the Day of Rest, they should all be confined within the four walls of their own Tabernacle, Camp, Church or Conventicle, whatever it may be, and those walls should be, by Act of Parliament, of sufficient thickness to prevent the escape of noise.

In one twelve-month period 669 Salvationists were assaulted, 56 Army buildings were stoned and damaged, and 86 members of the Army were jailed by magistrates. But the Army grew. In under ten years it had expanded twenty times over. The Army became respected and revered, perhaps because it backed up its noise with a great deal of social concern and action.

One of the Salvation Army's greatest processions was in 1885. It marched to the Houses of Parliament with a petition two miles long, bearing 343,000 signatures demanding that the trade in child prostitution (which was rampant at the time) be stopped and the age of consent raised from thirteen to sixteen years old. They succeeded and lives were changed. Drunkards sobered up and started to care for their

families; prostitutes gave up their ways and turned to respectable employment. Salvation had turned their lives around. A converted coal-cart driver summed it up. 'Well,' he said, 'no smoking, no drinking, no swearing, and the 'orses know the difference.' The world began to notice the difference too.

General Booth didn't see why the devil should have all the good tunes and the Army borrowed them shamelessly. This early Salvationist song goes to the tune of 'The Campbells are coming'.

The Army is coming – amen, amen!
To conquer this city for Jesus – amen!
We'll shout 'Hallelujah!' and praise His dear name,
Who redeemed us to God through the blood of the Lamb.
The sound of its footsteps is rolling along;
The kingdom of Satan, triumphant so long,
Is shaking and tott'ring and downward shall fall,
For Jesus the Saviour shall reign over all.

When the Spirit was poured out upon Wales in 1904, society could not escape its impact. For a time the courts had no new cases to try and the taverns emptied. A report read:

'Perhaps the most prominent feature is the lessening of drunkenness, for the night marches [converts on their way home from meetings] of praying and singing converts seem to have induced a considerable number of converts to abandon their evil ways.' Another commentator wrote:

'The revival of 1904 united denominations as one body, filled the chapels nightly, renewed family ties, changed life in mines and factories, often crowded streets with huge processions, abated social vices and diminished crime.

AND NOW – in recent years God has been moving inside the churches like an underground stream, bringing new growth and vitality. This is beginning to burst out. The church is becoming visible again. It has a voice which needs to be heard. The time has come to take to the streets again!

SO YOU WANT TO GO PRAISE MARCHING?

WHEN

Obviously, Saturdays are the most popular time, but some groups have effectively used Make Way on Sundays. One church regularly marches to morning service from homes in its area, covering a different route each time. Why not use the Sunday morning service as a 'warm-up' and process out afterwards. Fine summer Sunday afternoons draw a lot of people to the park and many parks have bandstands just waiting to be used (but investigate the bye-laws first – see the section on permission). Don't assume that open-air witness equals summer. Some very effective praise marches have been done in the winter, especially around Christmas time. Most Christmas carols have been around for a long while. See *Make Way for Christmas*.

WHERE

Shopping streets. These are excellent for maximum visibility, as long as they are not too busy. Bringing the town centre to a halt may cause a stir, but it won't make you very popular if you do it too often!

Pedestrian precincts. These are much easier, with no traffic control and noise to worry about. Some shopping precincts are privately owned so you need to get permission if you are going to be there for any length of time.

Housing estates. Only if there is good visibility from the flats and plenty of space to march. Choose a time when people are likely to be out and about (eg, not Cup Final afternoon). You could send a squad leafleting, either beforehand to warn that you're coming, or while the march is going on if you can spare enough people.

It is very effective to march between a series of suitable sites, such as the quadrangles formed by a group of high-rise blocks, stopping for a brief presentation in word, drama, etc before moving on. Don't outstay your welcome however, there may be some people on night shift who are trying to sleep! You could invite people down to watch and offer fruit punch or balloons for the kids, say who you are and leave a leaflet, including an address or helpline, inviting people to meetings. Note any 'warm' contacts for follow-up.

Around the perimeter of your patch. The good old Anglican tradition has a word for this! Rogationtide (five weeks after Easter) when you beat the bounds of the parish. The custom dates from medieval times when the whole village marched round to identify its boundary and 'beat back the devil'. Why not do it in song?

In Birmingham they have successfully organised an interdenominational march around the ring road, encircling the city with praise. They divided the marchers up into groups starting at ten different points and covering just over two miles each. Twenty-three miles in all – that's some parish boundary!

And also. The red light district, the village green, the sea front, council offices, tourist attractions, parks, slums, the centres of government and commerce. Wherever you need to declare the Lordship and love of Jesus – that's the place to do it.

Check there are no obstructions to your planned route.

As an act of witness the procession should be in a place where it is visible, audible, and will receive a high profile. This is not so essential if your primary aim is prayer. You should not cause any obstruction to the public right of way. Plan the route carefully, look out for obstructions which could slow the procession down or break up continuity. Will wheel-chairs and push-chairs make it? How long will it take? Processions tend to move more slowly than normal walking pace. Walk your route, time it, and generally check it out.

HOW

The method you use will depend on the size of your group, your resources, and your particular aims. Make Way has been done by anything between a couple of dozen and 15,000 people.

Companies. A group of anything up to 200 people can march in one unit, kept tightly together. Musicians can be in the centre, depending on the volume and clarity of the music. The more spread out the march, the further the music has to carry. Marching three abreast, for instance, creates a procession twice as long as six abreast.

Large groups may be best with a brass band in the centre or towards the rear of the procession so that the sound can carry. You could involve the local Salvation Army band, who would be happy to give you advice – they have 100 years of experience, after all!

Crowds. Larger groups than the above need to be divided up into clearly defined units with musicians in the centre of each. The people on the fringes of each unit may have difficulty knowing who to sing along with, so either leave a non-singing 'buffer' group between each bunch, or better still put a group of prayers between each musical group. Their job would primarily be to intercede as the march is progressing (they'd better keep their eyes open, though!).

Another method is to use a series of vehicles, wach with a synchronised sound system playing a *Make Way* tape for people to sing along to. It is necessary to use high quality reel-to-reel tape machines to get accurate timing. The tapes start together in synchronisation and then the vehicles move off at intervals. In order to cope with a march longer than twenty minutes, record the music several times over without gaps. The beauty of this method is that the whole march sings simultaneously, though the technical risks are

higher. If all goes well, by the end of the march all the tape machines are still synchronised to within a fraction of a second.

An exciting idea which may be worth exploring is using a radio link-up. Marchers carrying their own portable radios could tune in to a live broadcast. This depends on broadcasting regulations and policies in force at the time. Contact your local radio station and encourage them to give you some live coverage.

Do not stand too close to lorry.

Carnival style. Use an amplified band on the back of a lorry with marchers in front and behind. But beware! One group found the people immediately behind the lorry were overcome with exhaust fumes! Avoid hiring a smoky vehicle in the first place.

Two open-sided curtain lorries backed onto each other can provide a large effective stage area for starting and finishing points as well as providing transport on the march, with the added advantage of a roof

The police sometimes like vehicles in processions to move at traffic speed, so you may have to have the singers, similarly amplified, on other lorries. (Or else have them going for a praise jog!) If the police require you to move too fast, the music will not be effective.

You could march as part of your town's annual carnival, or make your own with a series of floats on a Christian theme.

You could use other modes of transport. One church used a tractor at the head of the procession, another had the vicar on horseback, one thoughtfully included a minibus for the old folk.

Converging. Why not have smaller processions from all over town converging on one central point where they can all join together in a combined act of worship? What more vivid expression of the churches' diversity and yet unity?

And then there's the Mega-March. Once you get into the thousands of people bracket (and we are beginning to see more and more of this), the planning starts to get rather complex. On a march of this size you may need crowd barriers, staging at each end of the route, extra public loos, and an awful lot of stewarding. Not something to be undertaken lightly, so make sure you hear from God before you embark on it.

NB: You don't have to have musicians. A proven alternative is to use *Make Way* cassettes and sing with them. These could be with car-mounted speakers (one small group just used a series of powerful car stereos with the car windows open), battery public address, or even a good quality stereo cassette player. To ensure a strong beat to keep everyone in time, a live bass drum may need to be added, the drummer keeping close enough to the sound source to keep in time himself.

You don't even have to march. Use *Make Way* on the move wherever you can, but where a procession isn't possible, use *Make Way* as a static open-air celebration in a suitable part of the town, sea front or park. Look out for local events which you could take part in, such as the village May fayre or the county show.

GETTING TO WORK

PARTICIPATION

Involve other churches in your area if you can. As far as possible *Make Way* should be an interdenominational event, a public witness to the unity of the body of Christ. Many reports of marches stressed how good it was to be working with other Christians in this way.

> 'Some important ongoing friendships have been established among the leaders who planned it, and people have been given a sense of corporateness, and their vision has been enlarged and challenged.
>
> It was good to feel a major presence instead of being a minority group.
>
> The thrilling thing about the whole event was the way the whole body of Christ came together .... We expected between 300 and 500, 700-800 came.
>
> It was fantastic .... To watch them turn the corner and see the banners and people praising the Lord was the most wonderful thing I'd ever seen.'
>
> *Salvation Army lady at North Staffordshire march.*

An interchurch march may take more effort, but it will be worth while. It will involve:

Planning – More organisation and committees will be needed. It may be good to organise rehearsals together, or a joint celebration where different groups can get used to worshipping and praying with each other.

Personal invitation – This is better than sending a piece of paper. Beware! Church secretaries' waste-paper bins are full of unsolicited bumph, so find out the person most likely to be interested. If necessary, be prepared to go along and explain the concept. Share the vision, let other people catch your enthusiasm.

Publicity – give full information and keep all concerned updated about the march.

> A twenty-minute training video in which Graham Kendrick explains the concept of *Make Way*, with examples taken from actual marches, is available for sale or hire (see Appendix C). People can grasp the idea much more easily by seeing it in practice.

PLANNING THE PROGRAMME

Make Way processions are designed for the streets, using a sequence of songs, shouts and prayers. Of course, additional material may be used in specific circumstances. The important thing is to make sure everyone is clear about which songs to sing and in which order they should be sung.

Music books are available with the basic piano part and guitar chords. Make sure your musicians have enough copies.

TEACH THE SONGS

— During, before or after regular meetings, at house groups, etc.
— By encouraging people to listen to the tape individually – in the car, doing the housework, etc.
— In special rehearsals.
— By rehearsing a core choir as well as the congregation. But don't let the others think they can come totally unprepared.

Encourage people to learn the words – it isn't quite so liberating to have your nose in a book. The songs should be familiar enough to people that they can go out worshipping and not be struggling to get them right. But in any case, make sure sufficient copies of the lyrics are available on the day. (See the notice on page 2 regarding reproduction of lyrics for *Make Way*.)

TRAIN THE BAND

Rhythm. A variety of different instruments can be used, but it is most important to have a clear rhythm. The big bass drum, carried by a strong person with a good sense of rhythm, is by far the best way of setting the beat. Add to that a snare drum or a side drum, suitably

harnessed, and you have a versatile unit. There is quite an art to keeping the right tempo and changing it between songs. If the drummer is unsure, a prepared cassette in a personal hi-fi, or a portable electronic metronome (common among drummers) could cue him in to the right beat. We have noted the beats per minute in the music book. Even during the gaps between songs, when prayers or corporate readings are taking place, let the drums continue. They announce the march from far off and maintain the sense of occasion. It has been observed that if a march lapses into silence, its energy and effectiveness quickly dissipates.

Guitars are fine, but their sound does not travel very well. Treat them as part of the rhythm section and keep them close to the drum. One 'first' guitarist could be amplified.

No independent tambourines! This is not to say that a well-rehearsed single percussionist or even a timbrel group cannot add to the music, but a rogue tambourinist can play havoc with the rhythm and cause a musical free-for-all – not a good witness!

Melody. The best way of carrying the melody is with brass instruments or wind instruments such as the flute and clarinet. Try and get a full brass band for larger gatherings. Brass parts are available (see Appendix C).

The shout leader. Obviously someone with a loud voice, but also with a good sense of rhythm. Place him near the drum and give him some PA. He could be combined with either of the two following roles.

The song leader. He must give a clear, confident lead and set the tone of the event. He must be able to lead the band, cue the songs, correct errors quickly, and keep the momentum of the worship. He requires a microphone – held by someone else or headphone mounted if he is also playing an instrument.

The prayer leader. People usually need to be given a strong lead, instructions, prayer points, and general encouragement to achieve maximum participation. Look for someone gifted to get people responding. Preachers and evangelists are often good in this role, musicians not so often! If there are pauses in the programme where people are unsure of what is going on, it will quickly degenerate into chit-chat. So be prepared to step in quickly.

One of these people should be prepared to give a bright and brief explanation to the public of who you are and why you are marching. Please avoid Christian jargon or you will make people feel more alienated. Be friendly, not aggressive or judgemental. You're sharing good news, not bad!

Rehearsal. Make sure the musicians are personally invited, competent, well-rehearsed and used to playing together and also on the move. Practise walking and playing in formation as soon as possible. Improvise a device for holding your music, if you need to (you could mount it on the back of the person in front). Cover it in a plastic folder to stop the ravages of wind and rain, and work out how to change sheets for a continuous series of songs.

If the band is on a lorry with a generator, you have the freedom to use more regular 'indoor' instruments such as a drum kit, electric piano, or bass. Rehearse in a similar space to the lorry flat-bed. Do you all fit on?

NB: Stopping and starting a lorry can be a violent operation. People and equipment need to be secure so that if the driver suddenly applies air-brakes the band does not collapse in a cacophonous heap! Going round corners can be interesting too. When travelling at traffic speed in a vehicle not designed for passenger use, certain safety regulations must be observed. Do not take risks!

Despite technical demands, encourage the musicians to worship. Try to make the standard of music as good as possible, but remember, as one group reported, 'It wasn't perfection or professionalism which made the impact, but enthusiasm.'

CHILDREN

Children are a major part of the church's life and witness, and should be encouraged to get fully involved at their various age-levels and abilities. They can learn simple dances, or hold balloons, placards or small banners. They can wave 'swizzle sticks', dress as clowns, and play ocarinas or recorders. However, do not underestimate their ability to contribute to the spiritual impact of the march through praise and prayer. As already mentioned, Psalm 8 reminds us of the powerful effect of children's praises: 'From the lips of children and infants You have ordained praise because of Your enemies, to silence the foe and the avenger' (Ps 8:2). Children's workshops and Sunday School activities can be used to prepare them for full participation.

OCARINAS

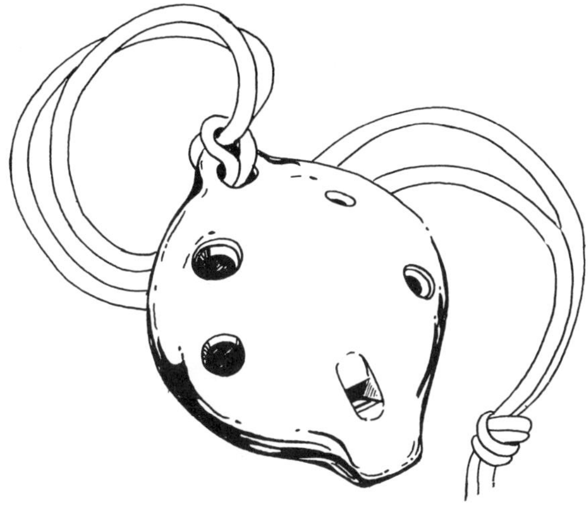

Ocarinas are small flutes that are easy to play and fun for all ages. They are worn around the neck as pendants and are therefore practical for taking on Make Way marches. The ocarina has a beautifully pure sound when played solo or in groups and is an attractive addition to any music or worship group.

Books with charts like the ones below help non music readers to play successfully in a short time. The Alto ocarina in D is ideal for adults and children alike. Ocarina music can be enjoyed by complete beginners as well as by able musicians.

Further information is available from The Ocarina Workshop, whose address can be found in Appendix C.

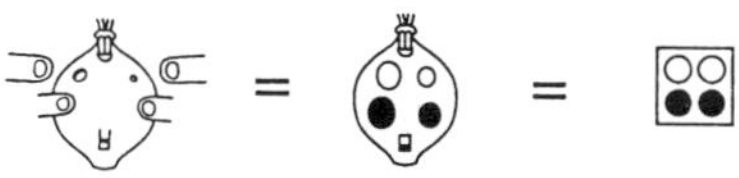

Shine, Jesus, Shine

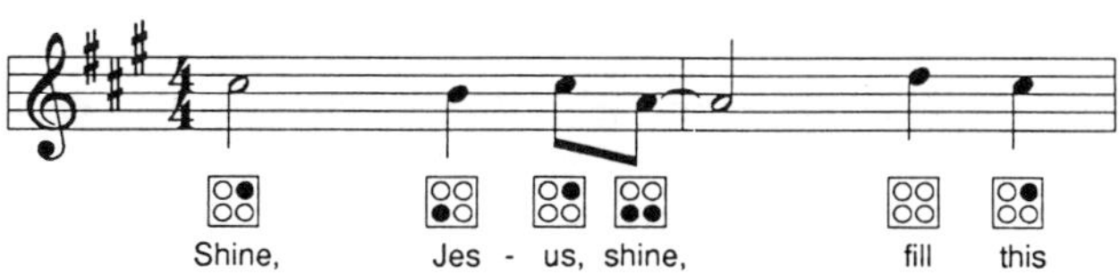

PUBLIC ADDRESS

You will need a portable amplifier capable of high-level output without distortion. Test for quality – some horn-type systems are OK for speech but terrible for music. It could be carried on a rucksack frame, in a shopping trolley, push-chair, pram or wheel-chair (but try not to let it look too silly). If using wheels, make sure the device can negotiate kerbs. Or be innovative – one sound system carried on the city march looked amazingly reminiscent of the Ark of the Covenant!.

You will need two loudspeakers, to point forwards and backwards. They need to be carried above the heads of the crowd, so mount them on some sort of pole.

Use a good quality microphone, and make sure you have a windshield. A quality megaphone is fine for spoken words but not ideal for music. But it is good for a stand- by.

PROCESSION ORDER

Are your batteries fully charged? Do you have enough to last the length of the march? Do you have spares?

If singing with a tape, carry a spare in case of failure. Run it simultaneously on a 'Walkman' player or something similar, so that if needed it will be roughly at the same point in the sequence as the first one.

A generator can be used on a lorry or at a static site. Be warned! They are noisy. Be careful! One keen musician borrowed a builder's generator and blew up his amplifier! An inverter can be used to provide 240 volts AC from a 12-volt car battery. Warning! It will drain the battery quickly. Lamp-posts often contain 13-amp sockets. Ask the council – they may let you plug in.

Above all, make sure you use well-maintained equipment competently put together, otherwise one loose wire and – silence. Try it out beforehand. Bring your sound expert with you on the march.

NB: Don't make more noise than is actually required, especially on a static site – it will not endear you to the neighbourhood.

For advice on the sort of equipment you need, go to a PA specialist. The names of some Christian firms are listed in the *UK Christian Handbook* (Marc Europe: Bromley, 1989). You may also be able to hire equipment if necessary.

POLICE AND PUBLIC HIGHWAYS

It is our right to hold an act of public worship in the open air, but our duty not to cause an obstruction or disturbance of the peace. It is the job of the police to decide whether this is likely. The 1986 Public Order Act has tightened up on the laws regarding marches, and the police now have more power to impose conditions on a procession, but only if they have reason to believe you may cause a public disorder. There is provision in the law for any conditions set down to be challenged, so make sure you clarify matters at an early stage.

In any case, you must write at least two months beforehand (preferably sooner) to the Chief Superintendent (Operations) at your local police station telling him what you want to do. Include the following information:

— Name, address and phone number of march organiser.
— Date of march, starting and finishing times.
— Assembly point, route and finishing point.
— Approximate number of people.
— Any vehicles involved – how many, what sort.
— Whether a meeting is to be held before or after the procession.
— What parking arrangements have been made.
— Name of person in charge on the day of the march and where to find him.
— Whether any organisation is likely to demonstrate in opposition!

You need not ask for a police escort – they will decide if it is necessary, and also the amount of police presence required. The police may be somewhat bemused by what you are doing, but they are usually very helpful. At one major city march, the police inspector told the organiser, 'This is your day, go and enjoy it'.

- Demonstrate that you are a well-organised and responsible group.
- Be courteous – the police have lots of other problems to think about.
- Be firm and persistent – don't take no for an answer, but be flexible and respect their advice.
- When discussing the route along roads, always try to insist on taking the whole of a carriageway in one direction. It's better than only taking half and then having vehicles scraping up the outside.
- Pray for the police on the march and give them plenty of thanks afterwards.

PERMISSION

Parks. Parks are usually run by local authorities and most have by-laws restricting the playing of music, particularly amplified, but they may well allow you if you ask. Chat to the park-keeper if you can, otherwise write to the council. Beware! it can take endless committees, so apply at least three months in advance. If you are a small enough group to be flexible, book several options – the weather may not always be kind.

Housing estates. These are the property of the local authority and technically their permission should be sought, but your request could easily sink in a sea of red tape, so use your discretion.

Shopping precincts. These are often privately owned. They sometimes have a manager on the premises, but may be run by an absentee property company. Either way, make sure they give you written permission. Managements are often amenable, especially if they think that more people coming into the centre equals more profit!

The way in which requests are put across is often the deciding factor. Present the event as something attractive, positive and as an expression of the local community. Stress that you are a local community group and that you want to do something positive in the town. It helps if you can truthfully say that you represent so many thousand local people, ie the total membership of the participating churches. Personal contact is always an advantage, so try to find out the name of the correct person to get in touch with and deal with them direct.

After the march, don't forget to say thank you, and clear up any mess you have made. This is not only a good witness, it may help you get permission next time.

PRESS RELEASES

You may wish to spread the message even further than the limits of your PA system by getting a write-up in your local paper or a report on local radio. Send a press release at least one week in advance of the event to *all* local papers and radio stations. Explain clearly who, what, where, when and why. Do not use theological jargon. You may know what 'claiming ground' and 'breaking Satan's stronghold' mean, but your local paper may put it as 'church take-over bid' and 'religious group say town is demon- possessed'!

If they do not send a reporter, you can send your report and even black-and-white photos after the event, but act quickly. Most local papers need their copy in on the Tuesday immediately after the event for publication on Thursday or Friday.

See *Your Church and the Media*, a workbook by Nigel Sharp (address in Appendix C).

PRAYER

This is the most important preparation of all. Without it, all the rest is worthless. Musicians, planners, dancers, banner-makers – only if all our practical activity is steeped in prayer will the end result carry the Spirit's life with it.

Before the day

- Hold special prayer meetings if you can.
- Make it part of your church's regular prayer life.
- Issue pointers to prayer with your in-house publicity material.
- Send everyone on a 'prayer-stroll' – pray round the route beforehand informally in twos and threes.

On the day

Prayer groups: immediately before the march, break the crowd down into small groups to pray. Put adults and children together, and mix people from different churches. Give specific items for prayer at five minute intervals to keep people fully involved.

Simultaneous audible prayer: another effective method of prayer is to get everyone to pray out loud simultaneously. Encourage them to pray in raised voices, not whispers, but definitely not shouting either. Make it clear when to start. A good way to introduce simultaneous prayer is to bring it in immediately after a worship song ending with a crescendo. Keep the instruments playing to cover embarrassment!

Call and response prayer: it is very effective for one of the leaders with a ministry of prayer to lead the crowd line by line in spontaneous or scripted prayer and declaration. Prayers need to be simple, energetic and to the point.

Prayer songs: remind people that they can sing their prayers, and where appropriate use prayer-songs.

Prayer scripts: it may be helpful to issue a leaflet for use during the march giving prayer information about the areas you are going through, even scripting additional corporate prayers to be led by the prayer leaders.

Prayer sections: sections of the march can be made up of groups of people with a ministry of prayer, possibly with no obligation to sing. They need to be well motivated and able to sustain a long period of prayer, preferably out loud. They can also serve as a non- singing 'buffer' zone between groups singing at different rates. NB: be sure to instruct people clearly in advance about how and what to pray as they march.

Prayer should continue after the event. Who knows what long-term repercussions will result when Christians step out in faith declaring Jesus as Lord? Pray it through!

MARCH ADMINISTRATION – SOME BASIC GUIDELINES

The amount of administration necessary obviously depends on the size of march that you are planning. The bigger the march, the more people you will need to organise it. However, keep your central organising group small, but make sure that all the areas you will cover during the event are represented. For larger events you will need to identify heads of responsibility and give them full freedom, but they must come back to your group with their proposals worked out in writing. Below is a list of different areas of responsibility. The number of people who take on these responsibilities again depends on the size of event you are running, so if you have a march of only 100 you will probably only need one or two people organising the whole event.

Event administrator. This person is in overall charge of everyone else. He liaises with the police, and stays with the senior police officer on the day of the event. On a large march it is useful to set up an office where he can be based and where communications can be run from. Don't position this office in a noisy place, such as near your main PA! This person also deals with public relations, and should know at all times who is in charge of what so that any problems that arise can be delegated very quickly. He must also thoroughly brief any leaders who will take part in the event but are not part of the planning group. However, remember that any instructions given on the day to leaders or the whole assembly must be simple and must be repeated.

Chief steward. On a large march this person should not have to do any stewarding, but co-ordinate all the other stewards. The chief steward should start the march and move with the front of the march. His team should be large enough to ensure at least one steward to every fifty marchers. These stewards are assigned to a particular group and should be clearly identifiable by wearing armbands or sashes. If you have stewards from a particular group, then if possible let them steward that group. Their main job is to stay with their group, making sure that they keep up the pace. If you split up at all you may end up with a bus in between groups!

March marshalls. These people should be placed at strategic points along the route. They can be used as markers for starting points on prayer-scripts, but they should also keep an eye on how the march is going. As stewards of each group pass by them, any problems can be relayed. On a large march certain marshalls could be in radio contact with each other and the main base. If this is not possible, then any problems could be relayed through the police, who should be with the whole march, and the main administrator.

Site manager. If you are starting or finishing with a rally, you will need someone who is responsible for your rally site, its equipment and lay-out. He can also be in charge of any staging, but for a very large march you may also need a stage manager. The site manager must also be responsible for the cleaning-up of the site once everyone has departed. (Make an announcement asking everyone to pick up rubbish as they leave.)

Press officer. You may need to have someone in charge of media relations to deal with the press and other media. Make sure that you tell the media what is happening or they might pick up misinformation from an unreliable source or impose their own preconceived ideas about the event. This person can also be in charge of informing other groups of what is happening. He should be available at the event at some obvious place, such as by the stage, to answer all media questions and explain what is going on.

Bit and pieces. Don't forget to inform people like the St John Ambulance if you are having a big march.

Keep the organisation of the event as simple as possible, and establish clear lines of communication. One of the first things that you should do as a group is to decide upon your route and then walk it, timing how long this takes and noting any obstructions like level-crossing gates, subways and bollards.

Don't forget to inform the police as early as possible, and also contact your local authority. When meeting any of these groups make sure you are fully prepared and know exactly what you want. Don't go alone as usually they will only meet you if you have someone with you. Make very clear who you are – most other marches are negative demonstrations, so they may view you in this way to begin with. If you are organising staging, or have a large public gathering, then you will also need to contact the borough engineers and surveyors.

At a large event you will need a full PA system. Get in professionals for this job and don't leave it to someone who may run a small PA in their church. If the people on the march cannot hear your instructions on the day they could all end up going the wrong way!

On the day of a large march make sure you stagger the arrivals so that you don't have pandemonium right at the start. However, don't assume that people will arrive when you told them to – they will usually turn up too early. Groups that are waiting for others to arrive can spend the time praying. Be careful when walking through traffic that all children are kept under control. Also, be diplomatic when walking through shopping areas and across bus routes. Do *not* stop to pray while on your march unless you are quite a small group. Get people praying while they walk.

Finally, expect that the event will not go to plan. Make sure that everyone knows who to relate to, and for what problem, when the unexpected arises.

MAKING AN IMPACT

'AWESOME AS AN ARMY WITH BANNERS'

One type of banner mentioned in the Old Testament was apparently made of some sort of reflective material, mounted on poles, which caught the sunlight and presented a dazzling sight to the enemy. In today's praise processions the dazzling sight we need to display is the word of God.

Banners also serve to identify us, primarily as Christians, but also as Christians gathering together from many different churches. One of the exciting things about a praise procession is the way it unites Christians from different churches, as together we make a stand for Jesus, and for his truth and righteousness. The scriptures and phrases displayed

MATERIAL AND SHINY PAPER

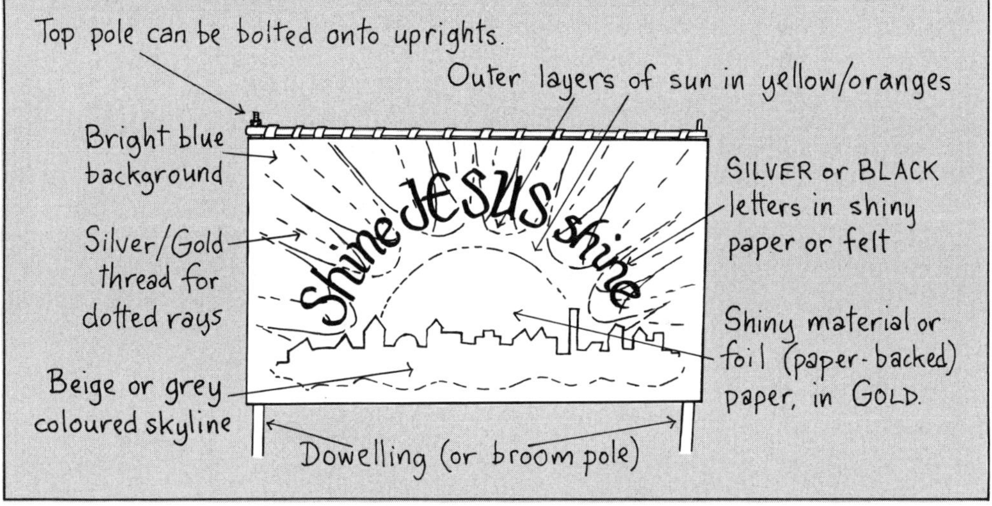

provide beauty and colour, bringing joy and life to our grey streets and creating an exciting spectacle to catch the attention of people passing by.

You may find the following hints helpful in making your banners:

(1) Remember that your banner will be viewed from a distance, so don't waste your time on fine detail.

(2) Unless well supported, large banners tend to crumple. Use plenty of battens and get some handy person to bracket corner joints. Bracket together pieces so that you are not trying to transport a fifteen-foot length of wood in an eleven-foot long car! Large banners also need a few carefully cut holes in them to allow the air to flow through when you are walking with them and to avoid being caught by the wind.

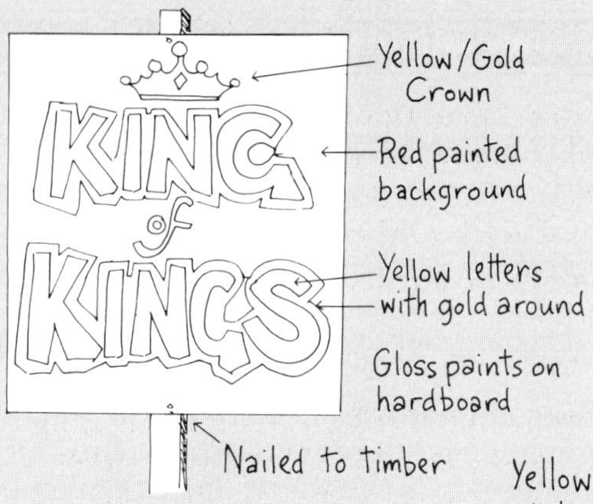

VERY SIMPLE BANNER USING HOUSEHOLD/CAR/ MODELLING GLOSS PAINTS ON HARDBOARD

ORDINARY HOUSEHOLD/ MODELLING PAINT ON HARDBOARD, OR ANY OF THE OTHER SUGGESTED MATERIALS

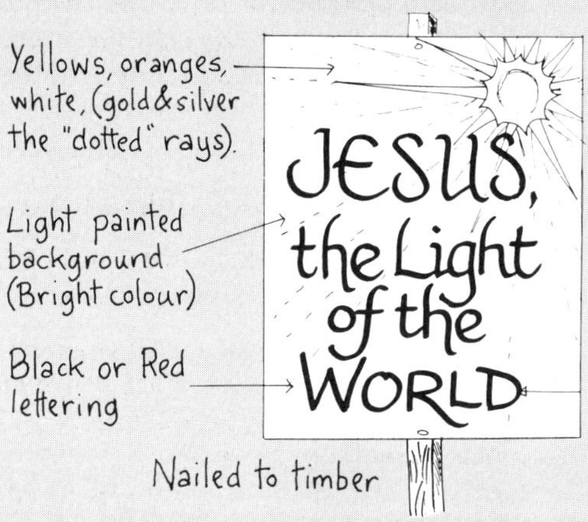

BANNER MADE OF MATERIAL, LIKELY TO BE LARGER AND THEREFORE CARRIED BY TWO PEOPLE

LETTERING SPRAYED THROUGH STENCILS ONTO FLUORESCENT CARD STAPLED ONTO HARDBOARD

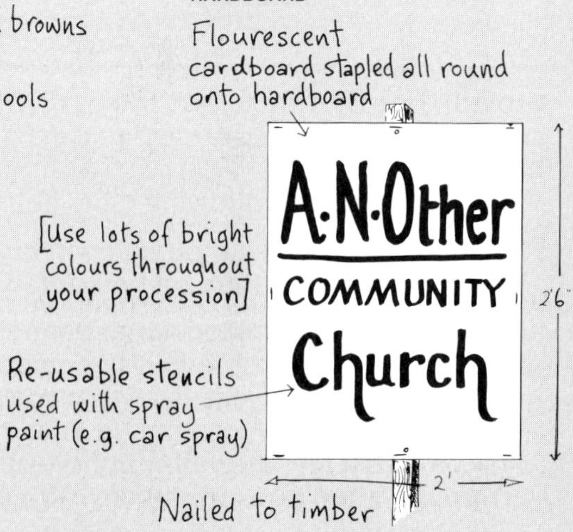

(3) Gloss paint on hardboard is very effective, simple and quick to do, and won't run in the rain!

(4) Spray your banner with waterproof fixer (the type available for shower-proof coats) if you feel your banner needs protection against the elements. If it is very wet and you want your banner to survive, you will need to cover it with clear polythene.

(5) Fabric paint is an effective and quick method for painting designs and lettering onto material.

(6) Lower-case letters are easier to read from a distance than capitals.

(7) You may like to try 'Spraymount', a spray adhesive available from graphic and stationery shops. This is helpful in fastening letters quickly as you can reposition them if you put them in the wrong place.

(8) Flag-pole carriers (your local Boys' or Girls' Brigade should have some) may ease the strain on the arms.

(9) You may find ideas for designs in the line drawings from the *Good News Bible*. You need to obtain permission from the Bible Society.

Balloons also add colour to processions and can be held in bunches and handed out to passers-by, especially children. Fill them with helium so that they float. Balloons and t-shirts printed with slogans are available (see Appendix C).

'Swizzles' can be made by taping strips of crêpe paper to garden sticks. Small flags can similarly be made using larger pieces of crêpe paper, perhaps with the words 'Hosanna' written on them.

Children will particularly enjoy these, although a little supervision may be necessary to prevent mortal injury!

Four metres of ribbon attached to a garden stick makes an effective swirling dancing aid. These need lots of space and are perhaps best used during a set dance when the procession is stationary.

CLOTHES

Dress the part. It is not much good making colourful banners if your marchers look as dull as a wet Sunday afternoon. Encourage them to wear bright colourful clothes. They needn't all look like walking rainbows, but just a splash of colour, like a bright scarf, makes a lot of difference. Why not have your own church logo printed on T-shirts, sweat-shirts, or even baseball caps? Make Way mailings give details of special sweat- shirts and T-shirts. Dancers can look very effective if all dressed in matching outfits.

Fancy dress. You don't necessarily want to look like a travelling circus, (even if people think you are!), but adding a touch of carnival atmosphere by fancy dress, especially clowns, gives the impression of people who are joyful and not afraid to have fun (for too long the caricature of the church has been exactly the opposite).

Use your discretion – if the prime aim of your march is spiritual warfare rather than witness, fancy dress will not be appropriate.

Members of drama groups could dress as characters portraying good, evil, greed, fear, love or sin. 'Perfect love' could have the job of chasing 'fear'! The characters could appear later in static street drama. Take care, however, to stay within the general discipline of the march.

OUTRIDERS

Make sure you have detailed a number of people gifted in personal evangelism to move along with the march, talking to passers-by, inviting them to meetings, offering them leaflets. If your outriders get left behind chatting, so much the better, but make sure you have plenty of others to replace them. Don't be surprised if people are prepared to receive prayer for physical, emotional and spiritual problems – after all, you have been praying for God's power to be released.

Outriders need to be people who:

— Are open to seeing God meet people's needs there and then.
— Are gifted in counselling (ie good listeners).
— Are able to communicate the Gospel in simple contemporary terms.
— Have a living testimony.
— Are equipped with literature for follow up, plus a pen and paper.

NB: This is not simply a job for those who cannot sing.

> On a more light-hearted level, your clowns might like to give out balloons (with a message card attached), sweets or badges to passing children – even adults may not refuse!

LEAFLETS

People are nosey! They will be wondering:

Who are these strange people?
Are they a protest movement?
What have they got to sing about?
Why are they smiling?

Don't leave them guessing. Use a leaflet giving the following simple information:

1) Who you are, ie the name of your church/churches, not *just* 'a group of local Christians'.
2) What you believe (briefly) and what you've got to sing about.
3) An invitation to regular meetings, or a special event after the march.
4) An address and phone number for anyone who wants help, counsel or Christian literature, etc.

NB: The first and fourth pieces of information (except the phone number) are necessary by law, and must be accompanied by the words 'published by . . .' The maximum penalty for infringement is £25 per sheet distributed.

DANCE FOR A PRAISE MARCH

Then shall the maidens rejoice in the dance, and the young men and the old shall be merry. I will turn their mourning into joy.
Jer 31:13 (*Revised Standard Version*).

Dance isn't just for the professionals, it is something that everyone can be involved in to show the joy and excitement in knowing Jesus. So let's get rid of our inhibitions and give everything we've got in worship to the Lord.

The march as a whole needs to contain as much movement as possible, with people clapping, waving, dancing and showing that they are enjoying themselves. If you don't have a dance group already, try to get together a group of at least six people who could lead the other marchers in dance. They should also work out more intricate dances for themselves to do during particular songs.

It is important that the dance group is prepared spiritually as well as technically. Dancers in particular are proclaiming Jesus, not only with their spirits and souls but also with their bodies. As they give physical form to spiritual reality they should recognise that dance can be a very powerful expression of spiritual warfare – see Psalm 149.

What to wear. Basically, clothes need to be bright and easy to move in, such as jogging suits. Jazz shoes are available from dance shops, but lightweight plimsoles are fine.

Dance routines – some ideas and starting points.

Jesus, He is the Light of the world. All the marchers can be involved in this dance. As the leader sings, simply walk to the beat of the music. As everyone starts to sing, continue walking and raise the right arm in front of you. The arm should be pointing straight up by the word 'world', 'peace' or 'God', and then lowered to the side. On the 'shout' phrase simply clap until the word 'Light', 'Prince' or 'Son' at which point both arms are raised straight up above the head in a sudden movement, and kept there until the phrase and movement repeat. These movements can be used for each verse.

Clear the road (*chorus only*). A minimum of four dancers is needed for this. Split them up into pairs, one pair placed six feet in front of the other one (this distance being maintained throughout the dance). The rear pair (B) runs past the front pair (A) to 'prepare the way of the Lord'. Pair A then performs the same movement during the next line. Pair B then repeats the movement again for the third line so that it ends up in front of pair A. Both A and B then turn on the spot to the last line 'of the Lord'.

The running movement begins with a small hop into the run. The body is curved forward and is straightened up as the arms sweep forward and then open above the head, falling naturally to the side. The hop and run starts on 'prepare' and the arms come down on 'Lord'. The pair that is not running forward walks in time with the music.

PASSING OPINION

'I think it's super.'

'It's different, very different – it's not really my cup of tea.'

'Rubbish.'

'They're singing in tune – that helps.'

'This sort of thing doesn't happen in Reading. Everybody's smiling – maybe they know something we don't. Everybody's just got big smiles on their faces. I never walk round Reading with a smile on my face, so maybe there's something I don't know.

FOLLOW-UP – Beware the 'Fizzle Factor'!

You march the streets, buoyed up with confidence, feeling like the mighty army the church was meant to be. You declare the power of Jesus, rejoice in His name – and then what?

You all go home!

This is what is known as the 'fizzle factor' and is to be avoided if possible. Your marchers are elated – they have discovered that it is not so embarrassing as they thought to have Aunty Flo and the milkman seeing them singing the praises of Jesus on the high street. The truths they have been proclaiming are ringing in their ears. There is a lot of potential energy waiting to be tapped.

HOW CAN YOU USE IT?

— Send people out in small groups to walk around the streets and pray for those areas.
— Have an open-air evangelistic rally at the end of the march.
— Set up several small open-air bases with street theatre, dance, testimonies, etc, and detail marchers to the different strategic points to pray, sing and witness.
— Send people out in small groups to give out leaflets in flats, shopping centres, etc.
— Have coffee ready at a hall near the end of the march and invite passers-by in.
— If you are finishing in a park, get everyone to bring their sandwiches and end with a picnic.
— Plan a special evangelistic event for immediately afterwards, or in the evening.
— If processing to a park, invite people to join the procession on the way. Have banners to that effect – this is great for holiday towns in the summer when families are looking for something to do.
— Even if your marchers just disperse, remind them to be open to the Holy Spirit. Several people have commented how unusual opportunities to witness occurred just after the march due to the spiritual atmosphere having been changed.

In any case, *Make Way* should not be used as a one-off event, but as part of an ongoing strategy for evangelism (see pages 49–51: Streetwise Evangelism).

Advice from the past:

'Experience taught that every outdoor service should if possible be connected with an indoor meeting – where, free from those dissipating influences which more or less always accompany outdoor preaching . . . the gospel could with greater clearness be set out.'

East London Christian Mission 1868
(*forerunner of the Salvation Army*)

STREET-WISE EVANGELISM

I have already suggested you can include a variety of ingredients in the procession programme. If you intend to end the march with an open-air meeting, or if you are performing Make Way statically in a shopping precinct, the following hints will help you know what to do and how to do it.

STRAIGHT PREACHING

Be succinct, and keep the presentation simple (two minutes).

— Make and emphasise one point clearly.
— Use short, catchy, pithy sentences.
— Be topical and relevant.
— Don't be offensive – share good news, not bad news.

OBJECT LESSONS

Jesus often applied spiritual truths from everyday items such as leaven, seeds, treasure or bread. Using familiar things to make a spiritual point attracts the attention of a passer-by and is more easily remembered than straight preaching.

SKETCHING AND LADDER WRITING

The street artist always attracts attention. Using the Open Air Campaigners' technique of 'painting with patter', there is time to put over Gospel truths while turning a simple ladder structure into words which visually communicates salient points.

PICTURES

For those with a little artistic ability, pictures mounted on cards work well on the street. Two or three pictures drawn in advance have a powerful visual impact. An alternative is to use a collage of newspaper or magazine cuttings.

ROLE PLAY OR DRAMA

Prophetic drama or role play was often used in the Old Testament, for example, Ezekiel lying in the street for 430 days. Modern equivalents can make an equally dramatic point, such as chaining your pastor to the railings to illustrate a person's need to be set free by Jesus. There are also many short sketches available for street drama.

LITERATURE TABLES

This can complement other types of open-air work or provide an alternative form of outreach. It provides free literature and a chance to chat. A large poster placed next to the table with a succinct immediate message can communicate as much as shouting with a megaphone.

TESTIMONIES

Interviewing an 'ordinary' Christian on the street can be less intimidating than a straight preach for both the interviewee and listener alike. Questions and answers can quickly get to the heart of the Gospel, using that person as the visual aid.

SOLOS, DUETS, TRIOS, ETC

The occasional performance song can add another powerful dynamic to the mix of items in an open-air presentation.

OTHER IDEAS

Puppets, banners, film shows (after dark), open-air services.

IMPRESSIONS OF STREET PRAISE

'A man who was standing on the other side of the road and had been watching, broke down in tears and got saved there and then.'

Watford, Hertfordshire.

'We were changed by the experience. We had started out as a rather nervous body of people, prepared to make the right noises but still with some nervousness. We came back and would have marched all round again and much further had we been allowed to. We had been made bold.'

Wimbledon Praise March.

'It was raining, but we all got together to worship the Lord, singing the praises of God. As we sang, a woman (by this time windows were opened all around us) suddenly left her room and ran towards us saying, "The Lord has sent you."

The songs were inspired. As she heard them, God began ministering to her. "What a joy," she proclaimed, "God is here. You people have brought him to me – show how I can know him now." '

Broadwater Farm Estate, Tottenham.

'I shall never forget the sight of every one of our 200 marchers dancing wildly to a Hebrew folk tune in the middle of a busy Welsh town square. Quiet ministers, old ladies, young lads – all praising God for Jesus. Abergavenny has never seen anything like it!'

Abergavenny, South Wales.

Make Way for Jesus

Shine, Jesus, Shine

MAKE WAY FOR JESUS

SHINE, JESUS, SHINE – MUSIC

Prepare the way
  (Clear the road)
Cry hosanna
Fling wide your doors
Jesus, He is the Light of the world
Raise the shout!
Creation creed
  (The Lord is a mighty King)
The King of glory comes
  (King of kings)
Lord, have mercy on this nation
I will build My church
God is good/Dance, dance, dance/
  Cry hosanna (reprise)
Light has dawned
Shine, Jesus, shine (reprise)

FANFARE

SHOUT

Leader: Make way, make way,
Response: Make way, make way,
Leader: For the King of kings.
Response: For the King of kings.

Repeat

Prepare the way
(Clear the road)

Capo 2 (C)

Graham Kendrick

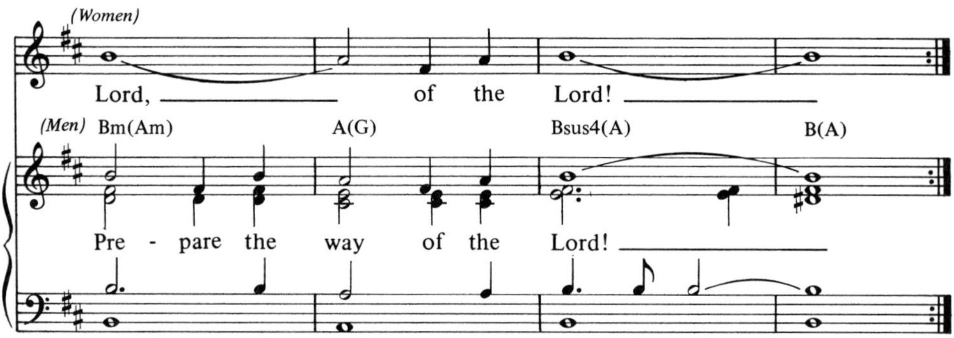

2. Raise Your voice and join the song, *(echo)*
God made flesh to us has come. *(echo)*
Welcome Him, your banners wave. *(echo)*
(Cheers, shouts, wave banners, etc.)

3. For all sin the price is paid, *(echo)*
All our sins on Jesus laid. *(echo)*
By His blood we are made clean. *(echo)*
(Cheers, shouts of thanksgiving)

4. At His feet come humbly bow, *(echo)*
In your lives enthrone Him now. *(echo)*
See, your great Deliverer comes. *(echo)*
(Cheers, shouts welcoming Jesus)

(Chorus twice to end)

SHOUT

Leader: Lord, we wel - come You!
Response: Lord, we wel - come You!

Leader: Je - sus, we wel - come You!
Response: Je - sus, we wel - come You!

Leader: Wel - come the King of kings!
Response: Wel - come the King of kings!

All: *Cheers, etc.*

Cry hosanna

Capo 2 (C)

Graham Kendrick

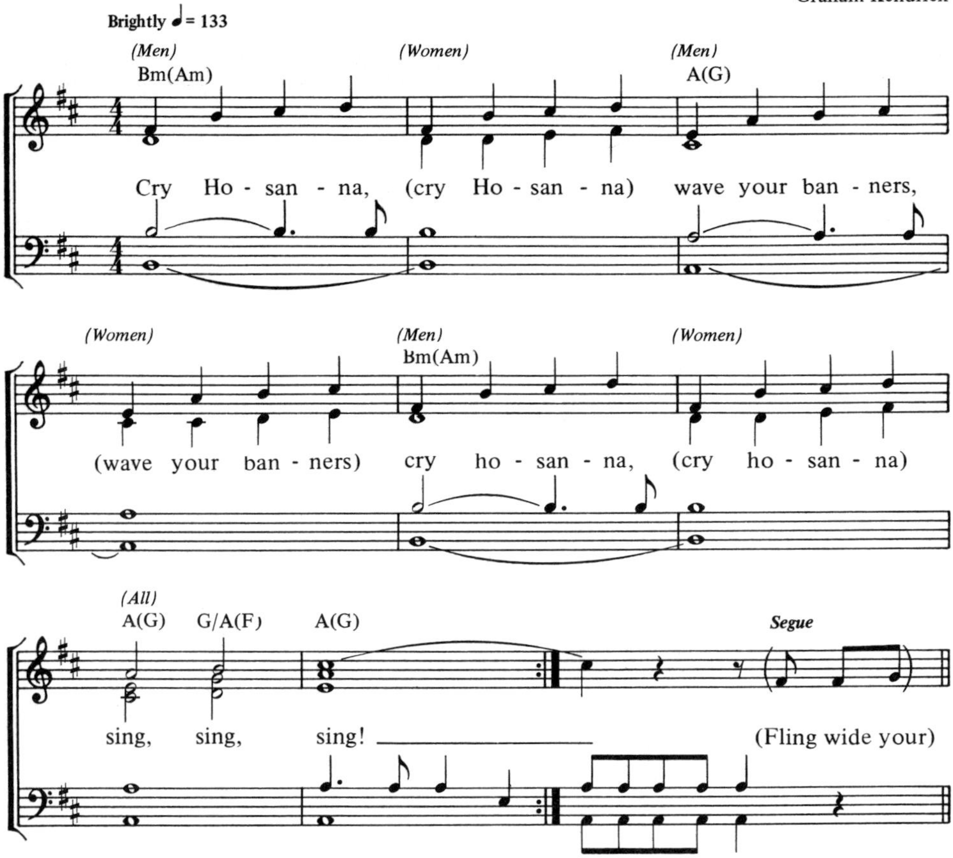

Fling wide your doors

TWICE; 3rd TIME THROUGH TO CODA

Capo 2 (C)

With vigour ♩= 133

Graham Kendrick

All: Great and wonderful are Your deeds,
O Lord God the Almighty,
Just and true are Your ways,
O King of the nations!
Who shall not honour and praise Your name, O Lord?
For You alone are holy;
All nations shall come and worship in Your presence,
For Your righteous acts have been revealed.
To Him who sits on the throne
And to the Lamb
Be praise,
And honour,
Glory and might,
For ever and ever,
Amen!

Jesus, He is the Light of the world

Smoothly ♩ = 86

Graham Kendrick

Raise the shout!

Graham Kendrick

SHOUT

All: Your kingdom come, Your will be done,
Here on the earth, as it is in heaven. } *Repeat*

Creation creed
(The Lord is a mighty King)

Capo 2 (G)

Graham Kendrick

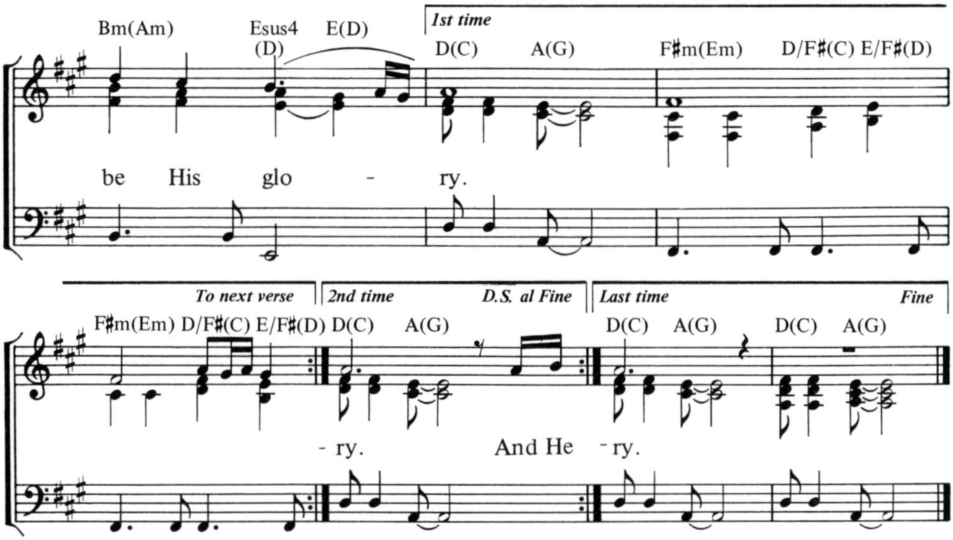

2. And yet we were deceived, *(Men)*
In pride the Lie believed, *(Women)*
To sin and death's decay – *(Men)*
The whole creation fell that day. *(Women)*
Now all creation *(Men)*
Yearns for liberation; *(Women)*
All things in Christ restored – *(Men)*
The purchase of His precious blood. *(Women)*

SHOUT

All: For by Him
All things were created,
Things in heaven
And on earth,
Visible and invisible,
Whether thrones
Or powers
Or rulers
Or authorities;
All things were created by Him,
And for Him.

The King of glory comes
(King of kings)

Capo 2 (G)

Graham Kendrick

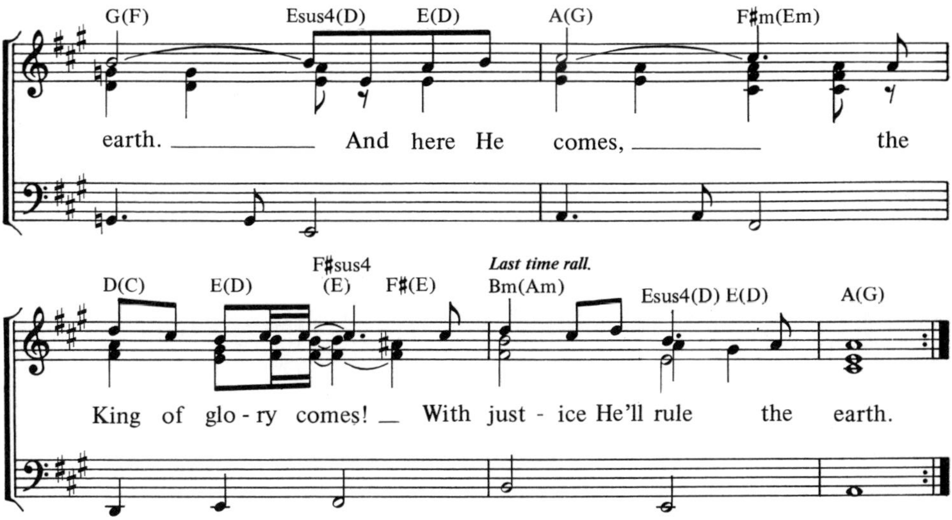

(Last time: Cheers, shouts of victory, etc.)

SHOUT

All: Almighty God, You are the Rock;
All Your works are perfect,
And all Your ways are just.
You are a faithful God who does no wrong.
Yet we Your people,
Both church and nation,
Are covered with shame
Because of our unfaithfulness to You.
We have sinned so seriously against You,
And against one another –
Therefore the foundations of our society crumble
Have mercy, Lord,
Forgive us, Lord,
Restore us, Lord,
Revive Your church again;
Let justice flow
Like rivers,
And righteousness like a never-failing stream.

Lord, have mercy on this nation

Graham Kendrick

SHOUT

Leader: Now Lord, send Your Holy Spirit.
Response: Now Lord, send Your Holy Spirit.
Leader: Drench this land with Your awesome presence.
Response: Drench this land with Your awesome presence.
Leader: Send Your Holy Spirit more powerfully.
Response: Send Your Holy Spirit more powerfully.
Leader: Let grace and mercy flood this land.
Response: Let grace and mercy flood this land.
Leader: Let mercy triumph over judgement.
Response: Let mercy triumph over judgement. *(Repeat)*

I will build My church

Graham Kendrick

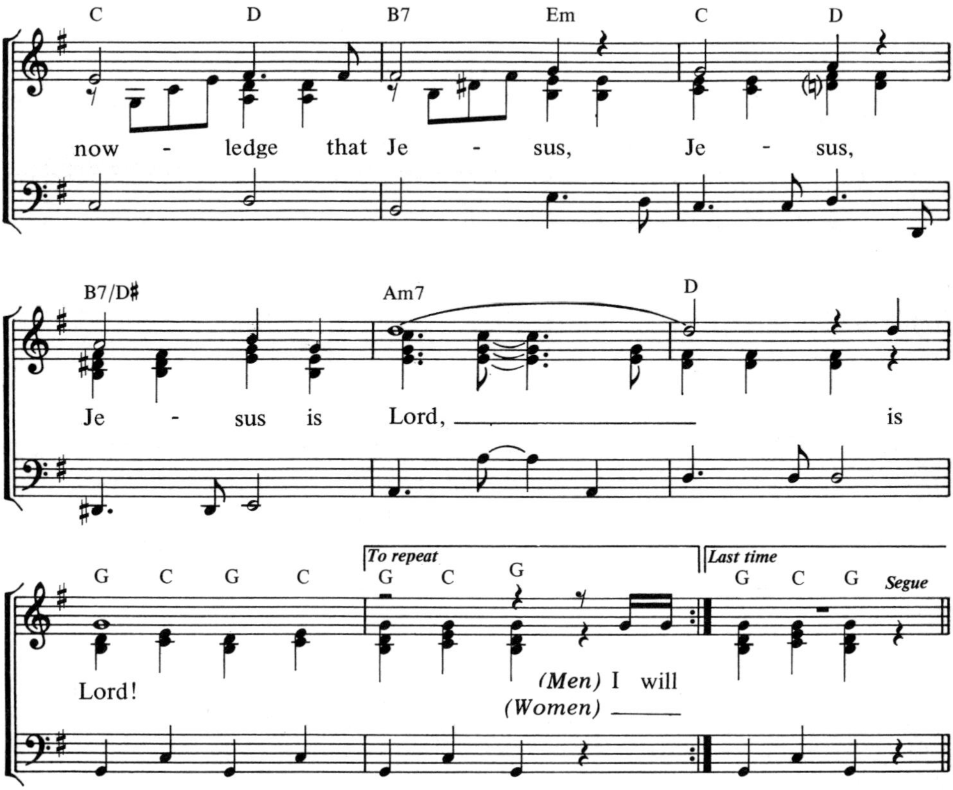
C D B7 Em C D
now - ledge that Je - sus, Je - sus,
B7/D♯ Am7 D
Je - sus is Lord, is
To repeat
Last time
G C G C G C G G C G
Segue
Lord!
(Men) I will
(Women)

God is good / Dance, dance, dance / Cry hosanna (reprise)

Graham Kendrick

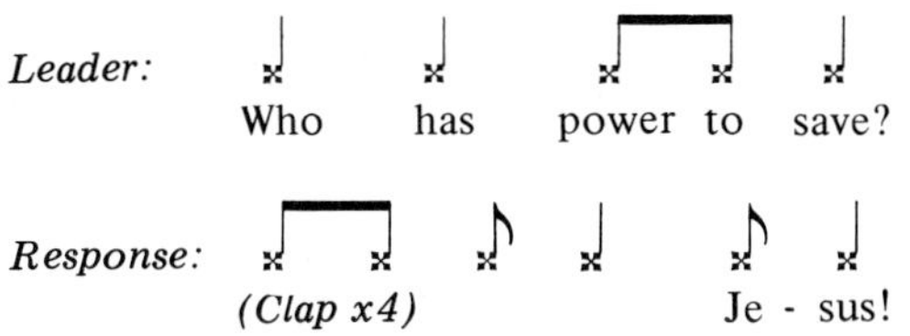

Leader: Who has power to heal?
Response: *(Clap x4)* Jesus!
Leader: Who has conquered death?
Response: *(Clap x4)* Jesus!
Leader: Who is Lord of all?
Response: *(Clap x4)* Jesus!

Light has dawned

Capo 2 (G)

Graham Kendrick

(Women)

2. Saviour of the world is He,
Heaven's King come down.
Judgement, love and mercy meet
At His thorny crown.

(Men)

3. Life has sprung from hearts of stone,
By the Spirit's breath.
Hell shall let its captives go,
Life has conquered death.

4. Blood has flowed that cleanses from sin,
God His love has proved.
Men may mock and demons may rage,
We shall not be moved!

(Chorus twice to end)

Shine, Jesus, shine (reprise)

Capo 2 (G)

Graham Kendrick

N.B. A longer ending to this song can be found on the recording, and more accomplished musicians or larger musical groups may wish to use that as an appropriate ending to their march.

SHINE, JESUS, SHINE – LYRICS

SHOUT

Ldr: Make way, make way
All: Make way, make way

Ldr: For the King of kings
All: For the King of kings

Ldr: Make way, make way
All: Make way, make way

Ldr: For the King of kings
All: For the King of kings

All: *(Cheer!)*

CLEAR THE ROAD make wide the way, *(Men)*
Clear the road make wide the way. *(Women)*
Welcome now the God who saves, *(Men)*
Welcome now the God who saves. *(Women)*
Fill the streets with shouts of joy. *(Men)*
Fill the streets with shouts of joy. *(Women)*

(Cheers, eg Hallelujah! God is with us! Love has conquered! Thank you Lord! Welcome Lord!)

Prepare the way of the Lord, (Men)
Prepare the way of the Lord, (Women)
Prepare the way of the Lord, (Men)
of the Lord. (Women)

Raise your voice and join the song, *(Men)*
Raise your voice and join the song. *(Women)*
God made flesh to us has come, *(Men)*
God made flesh to us has come. *(Women)*
Welcome Him your banners wave, *(Men)*
Welcome Him your banners wave. *(Women)*

(Wave banners, cheers, eg Welcome Jesus!
Reign King Jesus! Jesus—the Conqueror!)

For all sin the price is paid, *(Men)*
For all sin the price is paid. *(Women)*
All our sins on Jesus laid, *(Men)*
All our sins on Jesus laid. *(Women)*
By His blood we are made clean, *(Men)*
By His blood we are made clean. *(Women)*

(*Cheers, eg* Thank you Lord! I'm forgiven!
Hallelujah! Jesus—Saviour of the world!)

At His feet come humbly bow, *(Men)*
At His feet come humbly
bow, *(Women)*
In your lives enthrone Him
now. *(Men)*
In your lives enthrone Him
now. *(Women)*
See, your great Deliverer
comes. *(Men)*
See, your great Deliverer
comes. *(Women)*

(Cheers, eg Come Lord Jesus!
Jesus is Lord!
Jesus, Deliverer! King of Kings!
Lord of Lords!)

(Chorus twice to end)

Graham Kendrick.

SHOUT

Ldr: Lord, we welcome You!
All: Lord, we welcome You!

Ldr: Jesus, we welcome You!
All: Jesus, we welcome You!

Ldr: Welcome the King of kings!
All: Welcome the King of kings!

All: *(Cheers, etc)*

CRY HOSANNA, *(Men)*
Cry hosanna. *(Women)*
Wave your banners, *(Men)*
Wave your banners. *(Women)*
Cry hosanna, *(Men)*
Cry hosanna. *(Women)*
Sing, sing, sing. *(All)*

(Repeat)

Graham Kendrick.

FLING WIDE YOUR DOORS, *O you
streets,*
Open up you hearts of men,
That the King of glory may come in.
*Fling wide your doors, O you
streets,*
Open up you hearts of men,
That the King of glory may come in.

Who is this King of glory? *(Women)*
The Lord, strong and mighty. *(Men)*
Who is this King, this King of
glory? *(Women)*
The Lord, His name is Jesus! (Men)

(Sequence: Chorus, Verse, Chorus, Verse, Chorus)

Ldr: Fling wide your doors
All: Fling wide your doors

Ldr: O you streets
All: O you streets

All: Open up you hearts of men

Ldr: Fling wide your doors
All: Fling wide your doors

Ldr: O you streets
All: O you streets

All: Open up you hearts of men

All: *(Cheers, shouts, etc during and at end of instrumental)*

Graham Kendrick.

SHOUT

All: Great and wonderful are
Your deeds
O Lord God the Almighty,
Just and true are Your ways
O King of the nations.
Who shall not honour and praise
Your name, O Lord?
For you alone are holy.
All nations shall come and
worship in Your presence,
For Your righteous acts have
been revealed.
To Him who sits on the throne
And to the Lamb
Be praise
And honour
Glory and might
For ever and ever
Amen!

Ldr (Sings): **JESUS, HE IS THE LIGHT OF THE WORLD.**
Everyone sing,

All (Sing): Jesus, He is the Light of the world.
Ldr (Shout): Everyone shout!
All (Shout): Jesus! The Light of the world.
Jesus! The Light of the world.

Ldr (Sings): Jesus, He is the Prince of peace.
Everyone sing,
All (Sing): Jesus, He is the Prince of peace.
Ldr (Shout): Everyone shout!
All (Shout): Jesus! The Prince of peace!
Jesus! The Prince of peace!

Ldr (Sings): Jesus, He is the Son of God.
Everyone sing,
All (Sing): Jesus, He is the Son of God.
Ldr (Shout): Everyone shout!
All (Shout): Jesus! The Son of God!
Jesus! The Son of God!

Graham Kendrick.

Ldr: **RAISE THE SHOUT!**
All: Jesus reigns!
Ldr: Shout it out!
All: Jesus reigns!
Christ the fight did win,
Smashed the power of sin,
Love has broken in among us.

Ldr: Raise the shout!
All: Jesus lives!
Ldr: Shout it out!
All: Jesus lives!
He burst from the grave,
Now has power to save
All who put their trust in Him.

Graham Kendrick.

SHOUT

All: Your kingdom come,
Your will be done,
Here on the earth,
As it is in heaven.
Your kingdom come,
Your will be done,
Here on the earth,
As it is in heaven.

THE LORD IS A MIGHTY KING, *(Men)*
The Maker of everything. *(Women)*
The Lord He made the earth, *(Men)*
He spoke, and it came at once to birth. *(Women)*
He said, 'Let Us make mankind,' *(Men)*
The crown of His design, *(Women)*
'In Our own likeness,' *(Men)*
His image in every human face. *(Women)*

(All)
And He made us for His delight,
Gave us the gift of life,
Created us family,
To be His glory,
To be His glory.

And yet we were deceived *(Men)*
In pride the Lie believed *(Women)*
To sin and death's decay— *(Men)*
The whole creation fell that day. *(Women)*
Now all creation *(Men)*
Yearns for liberation; *(Women)*
All things in Christ restored— *(Men)*
The purchase of His precious blood. *(Women)*

(Chorus twice to end)

Graham Kendrick.

SHOUT

All: For by Him
All things were created,
Things in heaven
And on earth,
Visible and invisible,
Whether thrones
Or powers
Or rulers
Or authorities;
All things were created by Him
And for Him.

KING OF KINGS, Lord of lords,
Lion of Judah, Word of God.
King of kings, Lord of lords,
Lion of Judah, Word of God.

And here He comes, the King of glory comes!
In righteousness He comes to judge the earth.
And here He comes, the King of glory comes!
With justice He'll rule the earth.

(Repeat from King of kings)

All: (Cheers, shouts of victory, etc)

Graham Kendrick.

SHOUT

All: Almighty God, You are the Rock;
All Your works are perfect
And all Your ways are just.
You are a faithful God who does no wrong.
Yet we Your people,
Both church and nation,
Are covered with shame
Because of our unfaithfulness to You.
We have sinned so seriously against You,
And against one another—
Therefore the foundations of our society crumble.
Have mercy, Lord,
Forgive us, Lord,
Restore us, Lord,
Revive Your church again;
Let justice flow
Like rivers,
And righteousness like a never-failing stream.

LORD, HAVE MERCY ON THIS NATION,
For the sake of Jesus Christ.
(Repeat—First time only)
Cleanse us, heal us, save us,
For the sake of Jesus Christ.

(*Repeat from* Lord have mercy)

Graham Kendrick.

SHOUT

Ldr: Now, Lord, send Your Holy Spirit.
All: Now, Lord, send Your Holy Spirit.

Ldr: Drench this land with Your awesome presence.

All: Drench this land with Your awesome presence.

Ldr: Send Your Holy Spirit more powerfully.
All: Send Your Holy Spirit more powerfully.

Ldr: Let grace and mercy flood this land.
All: Let grace and mercy flood this land.

Ldr: Let mercy triumph over judgement.
All: Let mercy triumph over judgement.

Ldr: Let mercy triumph over judgement.
All: Let mercy triumph over judgement.

I WILL BUILD MY CHURCH, *(Men)*
I will build My church, *(Women)*
And the gates of hell *(Men)*
And the gates of hell *(Women)*
Shall not prevail *(Men)*
Shall not prevail *(Women)*
Against it. *(All)*

(Repeat)

So you powers in the heavens above,
bow down!
And you powers on the earth below,
bow down!
And acknowledge that Jesus,
Jesus, Jesus, is Lord, is Lord.

(*Repeat from* I will build my church)

Graham Kendrick.

GOD IS GOOD, *we sing and shout it,*
God is good, we celebrate.
God is good, no more we doubt it,
God is good, we know it's true.

And when I think of His love for me,
My heart fills with praise
And I feel like dancing.
For in His heart there is room for me
And I run with arms open wide.

(Repeat chorus only)

Graham Kendrick.

DANCE, DANCE, DANCE,
His truth has set us free.
Sing, sing, sing,
His song of liberty.
Dance, dance, dance,
His truth has set us free.
Sing, sing, sing,
His song of liberty.

Graham Kendrick.

CRY HOSANNA, *(Men)*
Cry hosanna, *(Women)*
Wave your banners, *(Men)*
Wave your banners, *(Women)*
Cry hosanna, *(Men)*
Cry hosanna. *(Women)*
Sing, sing, sing, *(All)*
(Last time only)
Sing!

(Repeat)

Graham Kendrick.

SHOUT

Ldr: Who has power to save?

All: *(Clap × 4)* Jesus!

Ldr: Who has power to heal?
All: *(Clap × 4)* Jesus!

Ldr: Who has conquered death?
All: *(Clap × 4)* Jesus!

Ldr: Who is Lord of all?
All: *(Clap × 4)* Jesus!

LIGHT HAS DAWNED that ever shall blaze,
Darkness flees away.
Christ the light has shone in our hearts,
Turning night to day.

We proclaim Him King of kings,
We lift high His name.
Heaven and earth shall bow at His feet
When He comes to reign.

(Women only)
Saviour of the world is He,
Heaven's King come down.
Judgement, love and mercy meet
At His thorny crown.

(Men only)
Life has sprung from hearts of stone,
By the Spirit's breath.
Hell shall let its captives go,
Life has conquered death.

(All)
Blood has flowed that cleanses from sin,
God His love has proved.
Men may mock and demons may rage,
We shall not be moved!

(Chorus twice to end)

Graham Kendrick.

SHINE, JESUS, SHINE,
Fill this land with the Father's glory;
Blaze, Spirit, blaze,
Set our hearts on fire.
Flow, river, flow,
Flood the nations with grace and mercy;
Send forth Your word,
Lord, and let there be light.
(Last time)
Let there be light.

(Repeat)

(All cheer and clap, etc)

Graham Kendrick.

MAKE WAY

Make Way for the King

A carnival of praise

Make way

Graham Kendrick
Is 40:3-5; Lk 4:18-19

To be shouted out before the song:

Make way, make way
(Response) Make way, make way
For the King of kings
(Response) For the King of kings
Make way, make way
(Response) Make way, make way
For the King of kings
(Response) For the King of kings.

2. He comes the broken hearts to heal
The prisoners to free.
The deaf shall hear, the lame shall dance,
The blind shall see.

3. And those who mourn with heavy hearts,
Who weep and sigh;
With laughter, joy and royal crown
He'll beautify.

4. We call you now to worship Him
As Lord of all.
To have no gods before Him
Their thrones must fall!

(Chorus twice to end.)

We declare that the kingdom of God is here

Graham Kendrick

Lk 4:18-19; 10:9

Last time Chorus add:

We declare that the Kingdom of God is here, ***(men)***
We declare that the Kingdom of God is here, ***(ladies)***
We declare that the ***(men)***
Kingdom of God is here. ***(all)***

Sequence: *Chorus twice, Verse,*
Chorus, Verse, Chorus twice.

Let God arise

Graham Kendrick

Ps 68:1,3-4

To be shouted out before the song:

Let God arise
(Response) Let God arise
And let His enimies be scattered
(Response) And let His enemies be scattered
Let God arise
(Response) Let God arise
And let His enemies be scattered
(Response) And let His enemies be scattered

Triumphantly

A Verse A7 A D
(Women)
The right - eous be
(Men)
But let the right - eous be glad,
E E7 A F♯
glad, let them ex - ult be - fore God,
let them ex - ult be - fore God, let them re-
F♯ Bm Bm/A E7 E7/G♯ A
O let them re - joice for the King
- joice with glad - ness, build-ing up a high - way for the King,
D.C. al Fine
Asus4 A Asus4 A Asus4 G7 A
in the name of the Lord.
rit.
we go in the name of the Lord, let the shout go up in the name of the Lord.

The earth is the Lord's

With strength

Graham Kendrick
Ps 24:1-2

Chorus fourth time:

And all things were made,
Yes all things were made,
And all things were made
For His glory.

Sequence — Chorus, Verse, Chorus,
Verse, Chorus twice.

We believe

Capo 2 (Em)

Graham Kendrick
1 Cor 15:3-5, 20-25

2. We believe He sends His Spirit,
On His church with gifts of power.
God His word of truth affirming,
Sends us to the nations now.
He will come again in glory,
Judge the living and the dead.
Every knee shall bow before Him,
Then must every tongue confess.

Jesus put this song into our hearts

Graham Kendrick
Jn 13:34-35

To be shouted out before the song:

Shout for joy for the Lord is good
(Response) Shout for joy for the Lord is good
He is just and true in all His ways
(Response) He is just and true in all His ways
Shout for joy for the Lord is good
(Response) Shout for joy for the Lord is good
He is just and true in all His ways
(Response) He is just and true in all His ways.

Capo 5 (Am)

'Hebrew' style, getting faster

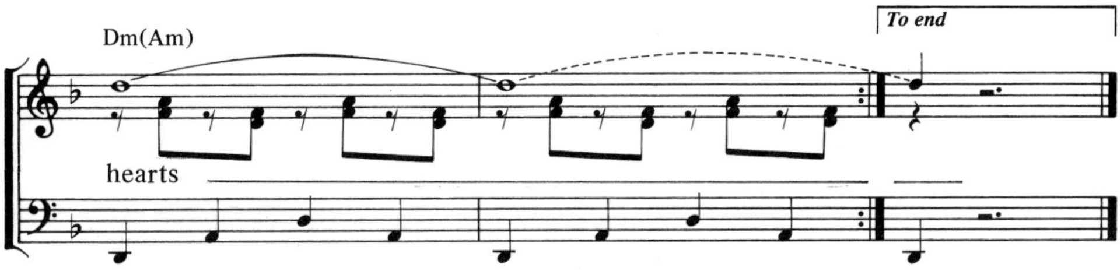

2. Jesus taught us how to live in harmony,
Jesus taught us how to live in harmony,
Different faces, different races, He made us one,
Jesus taught us how to live in harmony.

3. Jesus taught us how to be a family,
Jesus taught us how to be a family,
Loving one another with the love that He gives,
Jesus taught us how to be a family.

4. Jesus turned our sorrow into dancing,
Jesus turned our sorrow into dancing,
Changed our tears of sadness into rivers of joy,
Jesus turned our sorrow into a dance.

5. *Instrumental.*

The Lord is marching out
(O give thanks)

Capo 2 (Am)

Graham Kendrick

Ps 136

2. His army marches out with dancing
For He has filled our hearts with joy.
Be glad the kingdom is advancing,
The love of God, our battle cry!

Sequence: Verse, Chorus, Verse, Chorus.

In the tomb so cold
(Christ is risen!)

Graham Kendrick
Jn 19:28 - 20:31; 1 Cor 15:54-57

Triumphantly
Verse

2. Hell had spent its fury on Him,
   Left Him crucified.
   Yet, by blood, He boldly conquered,
   Sin and death defied.

3. Now the fear of death is broken,
   Love has won the crown.
   Pris'ners of the darkness listen,
   Walls are tumbling down.

4. Raised from death to heaven ascending,
   Love's exalted King.
   Let His song of joy, unending,
   Through the nations ring!

(Chorus twice to end.)

A CARNIVAL OF PRAISE – LYRICS

SHOUT

Ldr: Make way, make way
All: Make way, make way

Ldr: For the King of kings
All: For the King of kings

Ldr: Make way, make way
All: Make way, make way

Ldr: For the King of kings
All: For the King of kings

MAKE WAY, MAKE WAY, for Christ the King
In splendour arrives.
Fling wide the gates and welcome Him
Into your lives.

Make way, (Men)
make way, (Women)
Make way, (Men)
make way, (Women)
For the King of kings. (Men)
For the King of kings. (Women)
Make way, (Men)
make way, (Women)
Make way, (Men)
make way, (Women)
And let His kingdom in. (All)

He comes the broken hearts to heal
The prisoners to free.
The deaf shall hear, the lame shall dance,
The blind shall see.

And those who mourn with heavy hearts,
Who weep and sigh;
With laughter, joy and royal crown
He'll beautify.

We call you now to worship Him
As Lord of all.
To have no gods before Him
Their thrones must fall!

(Chorus twice to end)

Graham Kendrick.

WE DECLARE *that the kingdom of God is here.* (Men)
We declare that the kingdom of God is here. (Women)
We declare that the kingdom of God is here. (Men)
We declare that the kingdom of God is here. (Women)
Among you, (Men)
among you. (Women)
Among you, (Men)
among you. (Women)

(Last time only)

We declare that the kingdom of God is here. (Men)
We declare that the kingdom of God is here. (Women)
We declare that the (Men)
Kingdom of God is here. (All)

The blind see, the deaf hear, the lame men are walking,
Sicknesses flee at His voice.
The dead live again, and the poor hear the good news:
Jesus is King, so rejoice!

(Sequence: Chorus twice, Verse, Chorus, Verse, Chorus twice)

Graham Kendrick.

SHOUT

Ldr: Let God arise
All: Let God arise

Ldr: And let His enemies be scattered
All: And let His enemies be scattered

Ldr: Let God arise
All: Let God arise

Ldr: And let His enemies be scattered
All: And let His enemies be scattered

LET GOD ARISE,
And let His enemies be scattered;
And let those who hate Him
Flee before Him.
Let God arise,
And let His enemies be scattered;
And let those who hate Him
Flee away.

But let the righteous be glad, *(Men)*
The righteous be glad, *(Women)*
Let them exult before God, *(Men)*
Let them exult before God, *(Women)*
Let them rejoice with gladness, *(Men)*
O let them rejoice, *(Women)*
Building up a highway for the King, *(Men)*
For the King, *(Women)*
We go in the name of the Lord, *(Men)*
Let the shout go up *(Men)*
In the name of the Lord. *(All)*

Graham Kendrick.

THE EARTH IS THE LORD'S (Men)
And ev'rything in it, (Women)
The earth is the Lord's (Men)
The work of His hands, (Women)
The earth is the Lord's (Men)
And ev'rything in it; (Women)
And all things were made
For His glory (All)

(Last time)

And all things were made,
Yes all things were made,
And all things were made
For His glory.

The mountains are His,
The seas and the islands,
The cities and towns,
The houses and streets.
Let rebels bow down
And worship before Him,
For all things were made
For His glory.

(Sequence: Chorus, Verse, Chorus, Verse, Chorus twice)

Graham Kendrick.

WE BELIEVE in God the Father,
Maker of the universe,
And in Christ His Son our Saviour,
Come to us by virgin birth.
We believe He died to save us,
Bore our sins, was crucified.
Then from death He rose victorious,
Ascended to the Father's side.

Jesus, Lord of all, Lord of all,
Jesus, Lord of all, Lord of all,
Jesus, Lord of all, Lord of all,
Jesus, Lord of all, Lord of all.
Name above all names.
Name above all names.
(Last time)
Name above all names.

We believe He sends His Spirit,
On His church with gifts of power.
God His word of truth affirming,
Sends us to the nations now.
He will come again in glory,
Judge the living and the dead.
Every knee shall bow before Him,
Then must every tongue confess.

Graham Kendrick.

SHOUT

Ldr: Shout for joy for the Lord
is good
All: Shout for joy for the Lord
is good
Ldr: He is just and true in all His ways
All: He is just and true in all His ways

Ldr: Shout for joy for the Lord
is good
All: Shout for joy for the Lord
is good

Ldr: He is just and true in all His ways
All: He is just and true in all His ways.

JESUS PUT THIS SONG into our
hearts,
Jesus put this song into our hearts,
It's a song of joy no one can take away,
Jesus put this song into our hearts.

Jesus taught us how to live in
harmony,
Jesus taught us how to live in
harmony,
Different faces, different races,
He made us one,
Jesus taught us how to live in
harmony.

Jesus taught us how to be a family,
Jesus taught us how to be a family.
Loving one another with the
Love that He gives,
Jesus taught us how to be a family.

Jesus turned our sorrow into dancing,
Jesus turned our sorrow into dancing,
Changed our tears of sadness into
Rivers of joy,
Jesus turned our sorrow into a dance.

(Instrumental)

Graham Kendrick.

SHOUT

All three times: Christ has died
Christ has risen
Christ will come again.

THE LORD IS MARCHING out in
splendour,
In awesome majesty He rides,
For truth, humility and justice,
His mighty army fills the skies.

O give thanks to the Lord
For His love endures,
O give thanks to the Lord
For His love endures,
O give thanks to the Lord
For His love endures,
For ever, for ever.
(Last time)
For ever.

His army marches out with dancing
For He has filled our hearts with joy.
Be glad the kingdom is advancing
The love of God, our battle cry!

(Chorus three times to end)

Graham Kendrick.

IN THE TOMB so cold they laid Him,
Death its victim claim'd.
Pow'rs of hell, they could not hold
Him;
Back to life He came!

Christ is risen! (Men)
Christ is risen! (Women)
Death has been conquer'd! (Men)
Death has been
conquer'd! (Women)
Christ is risen! (Men)
Christ is risen! (Women)
He shall reign for ever. (All)

Hell had spent its fury on Him,
Left Him crucified.
Yet by blood, He boldly conquered,
Sin and death defied.

Now the fear of death is broken,
Love has won the crown.
Pris'ners of the darkness listen,
Walls are tumbling down.

Raised from death to heaven
ascending,
Love's exalted King.
Let His song of joy, unending,
Through the nations ring!

(Chorus twice to end)

Graham Kendrick.

Make Way for Christmas

The Gift

MAKE WAY

CONTENTS

Mary Evans Picture Library

I HATE CHRISTMAS!

There have been moments of frustration when I have been tempted to utter such words, and I am sure that I am not alone in this. I remember some years ago returning from a visit to India, and arriving two or three days before Christmas Day, and rushing out to buy some last-minute presents. The contrast between the pitiful slums of Bombay and bustling gift shops of the South of England was hard to cope with in the same twenty-four hours, and I found no way to reconcile the two extremes.

Yet love it or hate it, Christmas is here to stay, and if we can extricate ourselves from its more debilitating effects it offers enormous opportunities to announce the real good news, which is not how much people are spending in the shops, but how much God spent on us when he sent his Son in the likeness of sinful flesh.

MAKE WAY FOR CHRISTMAS

For those to whom the 'Make Way' concept is new, it is important that these notes are used alongside the *Make Way Handbook* in order to see its wider context and understand the practicalities involved.

Make Way for Christmas – The Gift has a few important differences. Side two of the album can be used on a street procession in the normal way, but it is also designed as a static event, indoors or outdoors. It is intended as the basis for a joyful Christmas celebration, a kind of Christmas party for Jesus, and it is up to your own ingenuity to adapt it for shopping precincts, churches, concert halls, schools, neighbourhood streets, carol services and so on. When used indoors, side one of the album is very suitable as 'part one' of a whole evening event.

As well as being a vehicle for proclamation, praise and worship, it aims to help us build a bridge to unbelievers for whom the Christmas story may be little more than myth and sentiment, a fairy tale with no relevance to the real world. However, behind the glitter and television glamour, the real world of Christmas is often an unhappy and stressful time for many people. It can become a focus for financial pressures, family tensions and loneliness, and the traditional over-indulgence and cynical materialism can leave people feeling very empty.

For others of course it is a happy time, but being temporarily happy is no substitute for being eternally secure in Christ's forgiveness. After all, the purpose of the incarnation was to save people from their sins, not just to make them happy.

Into this spiritual and often physical poverty, T*he Gift* is designed to help us announce the 'Greatest Gift of all' in an atmosphere of joyful praise. Many generations before Christ's birth, it was announced by the prophet that He would be called 'Immanuel' which means 'God with us'. My hope is that these songs will provide a framework for an *experience* of God with us as we invite people to join the 'party' that will go on into eternity.

Graham Kendrick

DID YOU KNOW . . .

. . . WHERE CHRISTMAS COMES FROM?

★ The birth date of Christ was not particularly celebrated by the first Christians.

★ The earliest record of a Christmas celebration is the second century when the second Bishop of Rome ordained that 'in the holy night of the nativity of our Lord and Saviour they do celebrate public church services and in them solemnly sing the "Angels' Hymn" '.

★ It was not until AD 336 that 25th December was fixed as Christmas Day.

★ It is likely that 25th December was chosen as a Christian counterpart to the pagan festival of the mid-winter solstice so that the birth of the 'Sun of righteousness' as the true Light of the world would be set against the *natalis invicti*, the rebirth of the sun half way through the year.

. . . WHERE CAROL SINGING COMES FROM?

- ★ 'Carol' means 'a song of joy accompanying a ring dance'.
- ★ Traditional carols have their roots in secular folk songs and pagan sources, and for this reason were outlawed from the Christian church for the first thousand years.
- ★ Saint Francis of Assisi plucked Christmas carols out of obscurity by his 'invention' of the nativity crib in 1223. Today crib services are commonplace all over the world.
- ★ Carols were sung outside and associated with drama and processions as long ago as the fifteenth century when the medieval Mystery Plays were at their height.
- ★ Carol singing and Christmas itself were banned by the Puritans in 1647.
- ★ Carol singing used to be called 'wassailing'. Wassail was hot spiced ale or wine which would be given as a reward to meandering minstrels and beggars known as 'waits'.
- ★ Carol singing from house to house as we know it only gained respectability in Victorian times and became a means of extending charity rather than receiving it.

YOUR FLEXIBLE FRIEND

There are many situations in which T*he Gift* can be used. Here are a few suggestions to get you started.

ON THE SPOT

High street shopping area

- ★ Find a site where you can draw a crowd.
- ★ Take care not to obstruct pavements.
- ★ Make sure you are not having to compete with other established groups – carol singers, charity collectors etc. Check in advance.

Shopping precinct

- ★ You have the advantage of a certain amount of shelter from the elements.
- ★ You must get permission from the management.

★ It will probably be crowded; take care not to cause a disruption. (NB: what you plan on a Monday in October could be chaotic on a Saturday in December.)

Neighbourhood location

★ This could be the courtyard of a block of flats, a village green, outside a local pub, railway station etc.

★ Advertise your presence in advance.

★ Have enough people so that some can go knocking on doors while others remain singing (see section on visitation – pages 120–122).

★ If you gather outside the pub, first check with the publican that this is OK.

ON THE MOVE

Procession

★ Will people be there to see you? Are you obstructing traffic?

★ Torchlight processions can be very effective at this time of year.

Carol singing door to door

★ This could be done as a one-off event or as phase two of a three-phase outreach. Phase one – put literature through doors about church and its activities. Phase two – carol singing, door-to-door visiting, offering personal invitations and Christmas cards. Phase three – church-based event.

Church event

★ Try to capture the party atmosphere – maybe a cabaret style with people seated at candle-lit tables.

★ Include drama sketches.

★ Church buildings are sometimes intimidating. Why not hire a social club, community hall or back room of a pub? Neutral territory can be less threatening.

Schools

★ Adapt *The Gift* as appropriate to the age group and situation.

★ Perhaps one class could perform it during assembly.

OTHER IDEAS

Once you have got your performance together, see if you can take it into hospitals, old people's homes, prisons and other institutions. Bear in mind that in some situations people will be disappointed not to hear traditional carols, so consider prefacing your programme with some well-chosen ones.

THE ACTIVITY SONGS

The basic level on which to use *The Gift* is simply to sing it, but it is really designed as much more than that. Many of the songs on side two of the album are designed as 'hooks' on which to hang practical activities, so that even if the words get lost across a crowded shopping centre, the ideas can still be communicated visually and dramatically.

Don't try and fit all these suggestions into one performance or you will be rushing around even more frenetically than the shoppers!

The simplest and possibly most effective level of participation is to encourage people to sing with you. Some of the songs have been written with this in mind, so make the most of it, and aim that people will go home singing at least one line of truth. Making printed words available will obviously help. Although *The Gift* can be used as a performance, ideally the whole church should attempt to learn the songs so that there is maximum participation and the whole event is not carried by an exhausted few.

'ARISE, SHINE, YOUR LIGHT HAS COME'

Light to a dark world is one of the strongest symbols of Christmas. You could illuminate this theme by:

Candles – Each singer has a candle. One main candle is lit first and the flame is passed from one to another to produce the effect of spreading light.

★ Cardboard candle bases can be obtained from church suppliers.

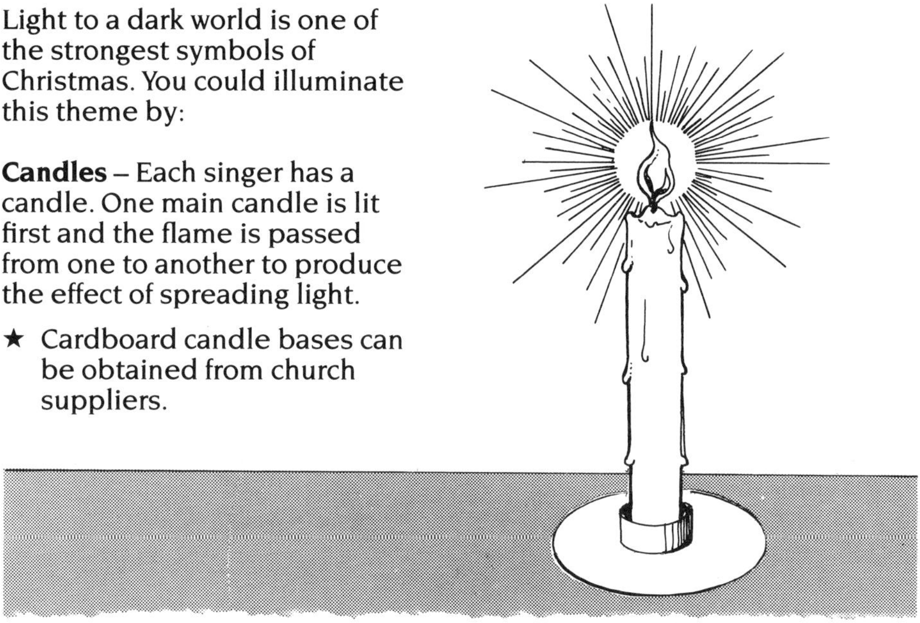

'THIS CHILD'

A nativity scene could provide a visual centre of interest. Remember this is a scene of poverty and homelessness, so try and avoid sanitised prettiness.

You could use:

★ a model, preferably lit up to provide a focal point. Candles or lamps could be placed around it.
★ cardboard cut-out figures – silhouettes could be effective.
★ real people and even animals. Eg somebody could play the part of Mary holding the Christ-child which could become the visual focus of this song.

'O COME AND JOIN THE DANCE'

Encourage people to join in the simple refrain.
Dance as a corporate activity is one of the most potent expressions of celebration. This song is in the style of an Irish jig, so why not make it one? Dance could be included in several ways:

Encourage willing bystanders to join in

★ A well-rehearsed dance group could perform it.
★ A children's dance group.
★ A simple dance that everyone can join in. Just 'one, two, three, hop' in a circle or in a line weaving in and out of the crowd would be effective.
★ Try and encourage willing bystanders to join in. Children will probably be most responsive.

'THE GIVING SONG'

Still a dance rhythm (Israeli this time), so the singers might like to carry on dancing while some of the following activities take place.

Drama
As a visual focus, have an enormous gift-wrapped box with words on it such as 'love', 'peace', 'joy', 'light', 'life', 'healing', 'forgiveness' and a tag labelled 'With love from God'. Build a short punchy drama presentation or mime around it, two minutes maximum.

Gifts

During and/or after this song, small gifts could be given to onlookers. Choose something that is inexpensive but has real value to the recipients and also some spiritual significance. For example:

Simple decorations

★ A fir cone sprayed silver with a ribbon to hang it on the tree.
★ A candle wrapped up with a message attached.
★ A balloon on a stick or filled with helium, with a printed message.

NB: gifts should come with a tag attached with a brief Christmas message or explanation of the gift. Eg 'As a fir cone is opened by the warmth of a fire, let God's love open your heart this Christmas' or 'This candle is a symbol of God's light in a dark world'.

Food

★ Sweets, mince pies, mulled wine, hot chestnuts – neither adults nor children are likely to refuse. NB: make sure your church insurance liability cover extends to giving out food – just in case you poison somebody!

Cards and invitations

★ A greeting from the church and a reminder of God's love.
★ An invitation – either an imitation one, making the point that God invites us to His party, or a genuine one, listing church Christmas activities.
★ Include a line drawing as a colouring competition for children to be judged at a Christmas service or event.
★ Cards and invitations for overprinting can be obtained from Christian Publicity Organisation (see Appendix C).

All tags and cards should display the name of the group and an address for further contact. (This is also a legal requirement for public distribution of literature.)

Announce beforehand the distribution of gifts; it will encourage people to stay and listen.

'FOR GOD SO LOVED THE WORLD'

Hopefully, the distribution of the token gifts will lead to a general 'mixing' time and some friendly conversations. Hence this song could be carried vocally by a core group of singers and musicians while others circulate. The mixing can then flow on into the next song.

Peace on Earth

'PEACE TO YOU'

Peace is in short supply in the run-up to Christmas – anxiety is more likely to predominate. Use this song to spread some peace and blessing around.

★ Move out and greet people in the name of the Lord, eg 'Peace to you in the name of Jesus'. On the streets, shake hands with those who have already stopped.
★ Offer to pray for them there and then if appropriate, or later. Perhaps you could even arrange a meeting for this purpose. Make a note of name and need. Follow up if you can.
★ Sing the song from your spirit as a deliberate act of blessing on the bystanders, passers-by and homes or shops.
★ Encourage people to sing it to each other.

'GOD WITH US'

The emphasis from now on is vocal participation and celebration in the atmosphere of a party, but beginning with this call and response song about God's closeness to ordinary people. Encourage people to sing the response lines and chorus.

'HEAVEN INVITES YOU TO A PARTY'

If you asked most people what word they associate with church, it might well be 'boring'. The idea of church as a kind of heavenly party is a surprise to most people, so let's give them a treat!

★ Get those feet moving, 'barn dance' style!
★ Relate to each other – don't just perform to them out there.
★ Use party poppers, streamers, party hats with 'Happy Birthday, Jesus' on them – anything that you feel is appropriate.
★ Beware, however, of alienating people by 'going over the top'.

'GLORY TO GOD' AND 'THANKS BE TO GOD'

Here we simply let loose in heartfelt worship and let God do the rest! The end of *The Gift* could be a cue for some quick-fire preaching or testimonies, for more worship, more 'mixing', or ministry to individuals, or to begin again. Beware of the 'fizzle factor' (see pages 47–48).

SIDE-SHOWS

To create a carnival atmosphere, try using some of the following ideas before or after your presentation of *The Gift*. (NB: 'carnival' derives from the Latin *carne vale* meaning 'farewell to flesh'. Make sure that even these side-show events have spiritual integrity and are not simply 'fleshly' activities.

★ **'Oh yea, oh yea!'**
  – Announce the performance with your very own Town Crier, complete with costume and bell.

★ **Chestnuts roasting on an open fire**
– Roast and serve your hot chestnuts, using a simple barbeque set.

Dress some of your people up in period costumes

★ **Puppet shows**
– Always a popular attraction with children. You could present the Christmas story simply and imaginatively with some well-made puppets.

★ **Instant photos**
– Dress some of your people up in period costumes, eg shepherds, kings, angels, even sheep, donkeys, oxen (or try live animals!) to create a realistic nativity scene. Then offer to take instant photographs of passers-by posing with the 'live Christmas'. You could even offer to dress up children to create more interest for the family album. All you need is a colour polaroid-type camera and... 'Smile please!'

★ **Slap it on all over**
– Painting children's faces with *washable* materials is another popular side-show. Alternatively, get children to make a hand print on a card saying '*Jason* is unique and special to God'.

★ **'Alas, poor Yorick'**
– There are a number of drama sketches suitable for Christmas. The sketch 'Away with the Manger' would fit very well with the nativity photograph session idea (see the book '*Scene One*' [Kingsway: Eastbourne, 1986], see also publications by 'Back to Back', 'Footprints' and 'Riding Lights'. To aid visibility you could perform your drama on the back of a flat-bed lorry.

NB: Remember that you need to obtain the necessary permission in advance to perform any material that is under copyright.

Or try live animals!

USING *THE GIFT* AS A NEIGHBOURHOOD STREET EVENT

In conjunction with a small neighbourhood procession, some of the marchers could break off into pairs and knock on peoples' doors to make personal contact. At a time when many households are fraught with tension and arguments it is a wonderful opportunity to bring the fresh hope and light of the Lord Jesus right into people's homes.

WHAT DO WE DO?

★ Greet with a gift or card.

★ Extend an invitation to a coming event.

★ Offer to pray.

★ Offer practical help where people are in need: but beware of making promises that you cannot fulfill.

★ Give literature.

★ D*on't* expect people to answer the door or to be very willing to stop and chat if:
– they are elderly or disabled
– James Bond is on the TV
– it is tea time
– only the children are at home
– you are looking at all miserable or sinister!

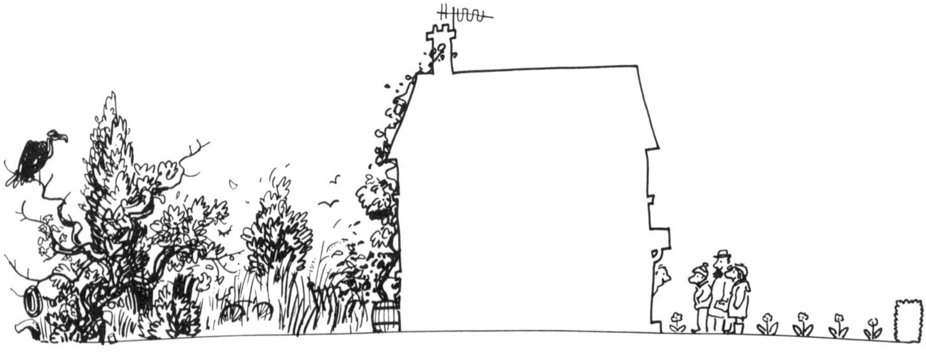

'Yes we'd love to do your back garden'

★ Do:
- give a friendly knock rather than hammer the door down
- pray as you go
- make a note (discreetly) of the address of people for whom a revisit would be appropriate (*don't* write an essay in full view of the next-door neighbour!)
- be friendly, natural, relaxed and avoid Christian jargon
- Smile!

Give a friendly knock rather than hammer the door down

WHAT DO WE SAY?

★ Introduce yourself: 'Hello, I'm Jean, this is Peter. We're from Parkside Christian Fellowship and we've come to wish you a Happy Christmas.'

★ Offer your gift: 'Please tuck in to a mince pie. Is there anyone else at home who would like one?'

★ Invite them along: 'You'd be very welcome to come and celebrate Christmas with us at our carol service, if you're not going anywhere else, that is. You're not? Then why not come along – it's just round the corner.'

★ Offer to pray: 'We believe God really loves you and cares for you. Would you be happy for us to pray a special blessing on you and your household this Christmas and for the New Year? We can pray here or come inside and bless your house as well (woof, snarl) – and your dog!'

★ Pray

General: 'Lord Jesus, thank you that you love Ken. Thank you that you want him to know your love and peace. We pray that you'll bless him and fill him with joy.'

Specific: 'We pray that you'll find him a job really quickly/ sort out his hassles with the rent.'

Direct: 'Lord, heal Ken's leg right now in the name of Jesus/touch Ken's broken heart and release Your Holy Spirit of joy and peace into his life.'

★ Leave information: 'Obviously we meet all year round. You'd receive a warm welcome to any of our meetings. Here's a leaflet telling you all about us and there's a telephone number there so you can get in touch if you need a helping hand or would like someone to talk to. Happy Christmas. Nice to talk to you. See you again.'

Clearly, you won't be able to go through the whole procedure at each house – that's a year-round job. But do go as far as you can in the time available.

Make discreet notes

FOLLOWING YOUR PRESENTATION OF *THE GIFT*

It is always good to be able to invite people to a follow-up event. Try to have printed invitations to give to people. These could either be produced separately or included in a Christmas card.

POSSIBLE FOLLOW-UP EVENTS

★ Videos for children, eg *Treasures in the Snow*, *The Selfish Giant*.

★ Evangelistic house-group evenings (more suitable after a neighbourhood procession).

★ 'Pay more, eat less' Christmas meal in aid of a Christian charity, eg Tear Fund, Christian Aid. (See Steve Chalke's book *The Cracker Manual* [Kingsway: Eastbourne 1990]).

★ Free lunch for OAPs on Christmas Eve, Christmas Day or Boxing Day – call it 'Room in the Inn'.

★ Carol service, or indoor performance of *The Gift* plus drama etc following an outdoor 'taster' of it.

Sample programme for evangelistic home evening.

Title: 'Neighbours' or 'Hark, the herald neighbours sing!'

Food: Hot mince pies, fruit punch etc.

Songs: Sing some traditional carols together for ten minutes or so (but avoid making non-singers feel embarrassed).
Perform some songs from The Gift.

Other: Ask a local person to give a testimony (five minutes maximum). A solo drama performance is possible in a house or flat. 'Stable talk' from The Riding Lights book Red Letter Days is suitable as it involves a cast of one (obtain the necessary performance permission first). This performance should last for five minutes. A short talk on the meaning of Christmas (ten minutes maximum).

NB: Don't trap people into an overlong event – watch the clock, and leave plenty of time for mixing at the end.

A similar programme could be used for a larger meeting.

I BET THEY HAVEN'T THOUGHT ABOUT:

★ **Keeping warm**
– Although your head might not feel cold, it is responsible for the loss of half your body heat, so keep it covered.

★ **Keeping the peace**
– Pick up any litter/leaflets after you have finished your presentation. Be considerate to the surrounding shopkeepers.

★ **Keeping people's attention**
– The concentration span of passers-by is quite brief on a cold December day, so keep talks and sketches short and punchy, and make sure each segment has an impact.

★ **Drawing a crowd**
– Use the 'rent-a-crowd' technique of having some of your own group forming an interested-looking audience. This not only helps to draw others in, but also avoids the 'us-and-them' syndrome.

★ **Coping with the music**
– If you don't have sufficient musicians to play the songs live, backing tracks for *The Gift* are available from the 'Make Way' address given in Appendix C.
– Have at least one keyboard player as a back-up to cover possible PA problems, to extend any section while the backing track is on 'pause', or to lead a few traditional carols while preparations are being made.
– Any accompanying instruments would need to be tuned to the tape before the presentation begins.
– If you wish to interrupt the programme at any stage, for example to give out gifts, have somebody ready to hit the 'pause' button at the appropriate moment.

★ **Using less conventional instruments**
– Piano accordions lend a certain attraction to a music group. The sound carries well in the open air and they are very versatile.
– Sleigh bells are of course the most Christmasy sounding instruments – but don't overdo it.
– Some of the songs are 'ocarina compatible'.
– At Christmas, of all times of the year, the local Salvation Army Band would be a particularly popular addition to your musical ensemble.

OTHER POINTS TO CONSIDER:

★ **Collecting money**
– Many people will expect you to be collecting money, and their discovery that you are actually giving something away may make a strong point. However, if for some reason you are going to

Mary Evans Picture Library

associate the event with collecting money, we advise you to write to Tear Fund (address in Appendix C) for a leaflet regarding the legalities of door-to-door charity collecting. Please also bear the following points in mind:

– Don't collect money and offer prayer at the same time. People don't have to pay to receive a blessing from God!
– Avoid making the whole presentation seem like a fund-raising event.

★ **Avoid secular symbols**

– Mistletoe is a plant said to have miraculous healing powers and is a symbol of fertility.
– The yule log was burned to honour the ancient gods who ordered the movements of the sun.
– Santa Claus (Saint Nicholas) does at least have Christian roots, but he will probably be down the road at the department store anyway.

PLANNING CHECKLIST

The following is a countdown checklist to help you organise your event based on *The Gift*.

SEPTEMBER
- Decide on the type of event.
- Start to inform other churches if you are involving them.
- If you want to use shopping precincts or parks, write official letters asking for permission.
- If you want to use a hall, book it now.
- Pray!

OCTOBER
- Choir, musicians and congregations should start to learn songs.
- If you are going to be on public highways, inform the police.
- Delegate people to be in charge of banners, refreshments, gifts, drama, dance, other props, public address, side-shows, publicity etc.
- Order or print cards and invitations now.
- Pray!

NOVEMBER
- Rehearse dance, drama and songs.
- Make banners.
- If you are using advance publicity, get it out now.
- Fill in the performance permission form and send it off to the 'Make Way Music' office.
- Issue press release to the local paper.
- Pray!

DECEMBER
- Collect the printing.
- Bake the mince pies.
- Blow up the balloons.
- Pray!
- Decorate the venue if appropriate.
- Go for it!

JANUARY, FEBRUARY, MARCH
- Keep on praying.
- Follow up contacts.

BANNERS – BRIGHTEST AND BEST!

Banners are the first thing that people will see as they approach your group. Make one banner with the name of your church on it. Make others on Christmas themes. For example:

★ Happy birthday, Jesus.

★ Jesus – God's gift to us.

★ Jesus came to pay our debt (over huge Visa symbol).

★ Jesus – Access to heaven (over huge Access symbol).

★ Happy Jesus Christ-mas.

★ Arise, shine, your Light has come.

★ God is down to earth.

★ Just like you – God spent everything He had.

★ Glory to God and peace on earth.

★ Peace to you.

★ Eat, drink and be merry, for tomorrow . . .?

★ Titles of Jesus: Wonderful Counsellor, Prince of peace, Mighty God, Lamb of God, Light of the world, God with us etc.

★ Familiar lines from carols:
– 'Light and life to all He brings.'
– 'Born that man no more may die.'
– 'Love came down at Christmas.'
– 'O come let us adore Him – Christ the Lord.'

Create 'rays of light' using bright yellow felt for the longer rays with orange netting over the top for the shorter ones.

If you are planning a static event, make the banner poles long enough to rest on the ground so you need not carry their weight.

Dark blue wording on a light blue background. Star to be gold shiny material. Grey felt illustration.

Other visual ideas

★ Lanterns (real or mock).

★ Streamers made of crêpe paper or lametta attached to sticks.

★ Balloons on sticks or filled with helium.

★ Lots of small star-shaped placards with names of Jesus, or 'love', 'joy', 'peace' etc on them.

★ Wear your brightest woolly scarves and hats.

Lots more practical information on planning outdoor events is found in the *Make Way Handbook* see pages 27–47. This section is designed to be used in conjunction with it.

ENTITLING YOUR EVENT

Although the title 'Make Way for Christmas' may be meaningful in Christian circles, it may not be outside. Hence it is suggested that when the event is being advertised for non-Christians, the title 'The Gift' is used as the main title, and 'Make Way for Christmas' as a sub-title.

Please do not entitle your performance 'Make Way – The Gift' if you are using substantial additional materials.

SHARING THE GIFT – MUSIC

Introduction (Good news)
Good news
Sing all the earth
Gloria
Arise, shine
This Child
O come and join the dance
The Giving Song
For God so loved the world
Peace to you
God with us
Heaven invites you to a party
Tonight (reprise)
Thanks be to God (reprise)

Introduction
(Good news)

Graham Kendrick

As a fanfare

Good news

Graham Kendrick

2. Let earth's dark shadows fly away,
Alleluia!
In Christ has dawned an endless day,
Alleluia!

3. Now God with us on earth resides,
Alleluia!
And heaven's door is open wide,
Alleluia!

Sing all the earth

Graham Kendrick

Quieter, same speed

Gloria

G. R. Woodward (1848-1934)

Music: 16th century French melody.

Arise, shine
(Darkness like a shroud)

Capo 5 (C)

Graham Kendrick

E (C) G♯m (Em) C♯m (Am) B (G) C♯m (Am) A (F) E/A (C)
- rise, shine, your light has come, the glo-ry of the Lord has
A (F) E (C) G♯m (Em) C♯m (Am) B (G) Amaj7 (F)
ris'n on you! A - rise, shine, your light has come,
Second time to Coda
A♯dim (F♯dim) E/B (C) G♯m (Em) A (F) A/B (F) E (C)
Je-sus the Light of the world has come.
CODA
E/B (C) G♯m (Em) A (F) A♯dim (F♯dim) E/B (C) G♯m (Em) A (F) A♯dim (F♯dim)
Light of the world, Je-sus the Light of the world, Je - sus the
E/B (C) G♯m (Em) A (F) A/B (F) E (C) Esus4 (C) E (C)
Light of the world has come! (Men) Your light has

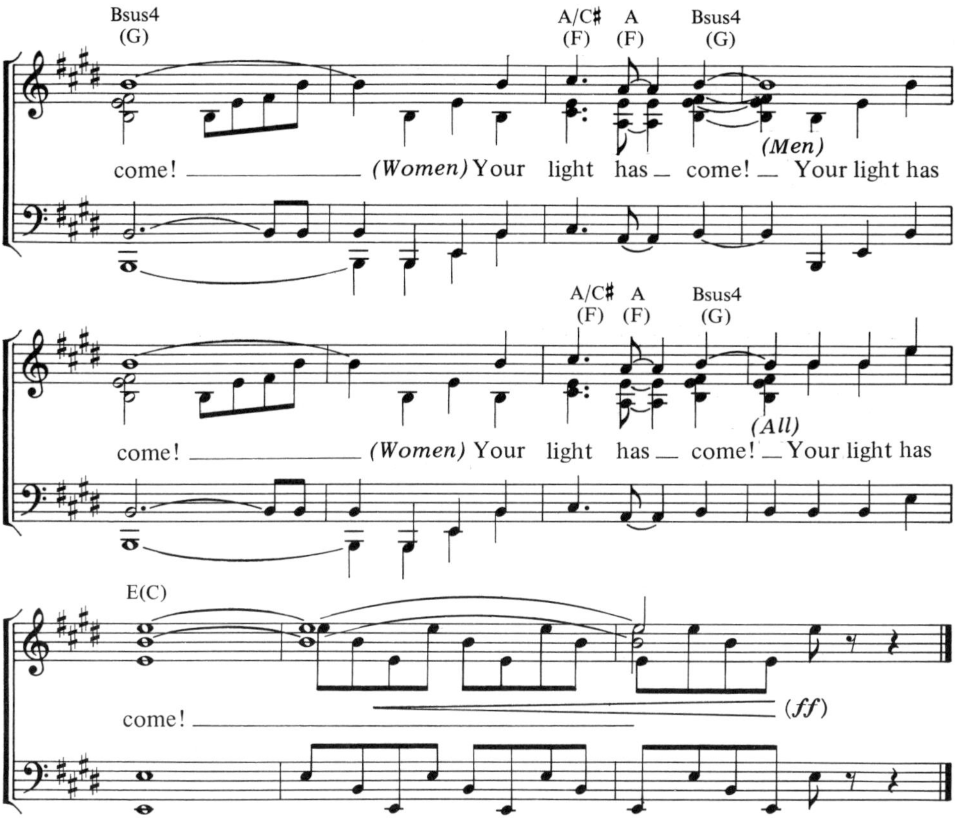

All: Cheers, etc.

2. Here among us now, Christ the Light
   Kindles brighter flames in our trembling hearts!
   Living Word, our Lamp, come guide our feet
   As we walk as one in light and peace,
   'Till justice and truth shine like the sun.

(Final Chorus)
Jesus the Light of the world,
Jesus the Light of the world,
Jesus the Light of the world has come!

Women: Your light has come!
Men: Your light has come!
Women: Your light has come!
Men: Your light has come!
All: Your light has come!

Leader says:
Welcome to the celebration! Welcome to the greatest birthday party of all time! We are celebrating the birth of a Child whose coming changed the whole course of human history, and who has changed our lives too. Though His arrival was almost unnoticed, His birth had been prophesied centuries before when the prophet Isaiah said:

All say:
For a Child will be born to us, a Son will be given to us; and He will be our ruler. He will be called Wonderful Counsellor, Mighty God, Eternal Father, Prince of Peace.

Leader says:
Let's celebrate together this most joyful of all birthdays, the birthday of Jesus, the Child from heaven.

This Child

Graham Kendrick

2. This Child, rising on us like the sun,
   Oh this Child, given to light everyone,
   Oh this Child, guiding our feet on the pathway
   To peace on earth.

3. This Child, raising the humble and poor,
   Oh this Child, making the proud ones to fall;
   This Child, filling the hungry with good things,
   This heavenly Child.

Leader says:
The birth of a child should always be the cause of great rejoicing, but how much more so when the Child is none other than God Himself, come to save His people from their sins! So come and join the dance!

O come and join the dance

Graham Kendrick

Am7
A7
-joice! Re-joice!
(Women) Re-joice! Re-joice!
(All) O lift your voice and sing, and
D
Am7
D C/D D
o - pen up your heart to wel-come Him.
(Men) Re -
Am7
A7
- joice! Re-joice!
(Women) Re-joice! Re-joice!
(All) and wel-come now your King, for
D
Am7
1st, 2nd & 3rd times
D C/D D
Christ the Lord was born in Beth - le - hem.
Leader
2. Come
3.
4. Let
4th time
D C/D D
D.S.
5th time
D C/D D
Am7
- hem. (Men) Re - - hem. For Christ the Lord was born in Beth - le -
(mp)

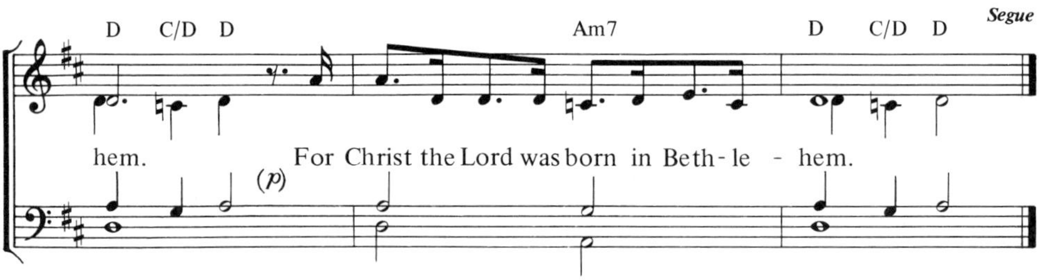

2. (Leader) Come shed your heavy load
And dance your worries all away,
(All) For Christ the Lord was born in Bethlehem.
(Leader) He came to break the power of sin
And turn your night to day,
(All) Oh, take my hand and come and join the song.

3. *(Instrumental verse and chorus)*

4. (Leader) Let laughter ring and angels sing
And joy be all around,
(All) For Christ the Lord was born in Bethlehem.
(Leader) And if you seek with all your heart
He surely can be found,
(All) Oh, take my hand and come and join the song.

Leader says over introduction:
On that first Christmas night, joyful angels announced peace and goodwill to the world—and heaven is still bursting at the seams with good gifts for everyone. So open your heart to receive what God has stored up for you, especially the greatest Gift of all . . .

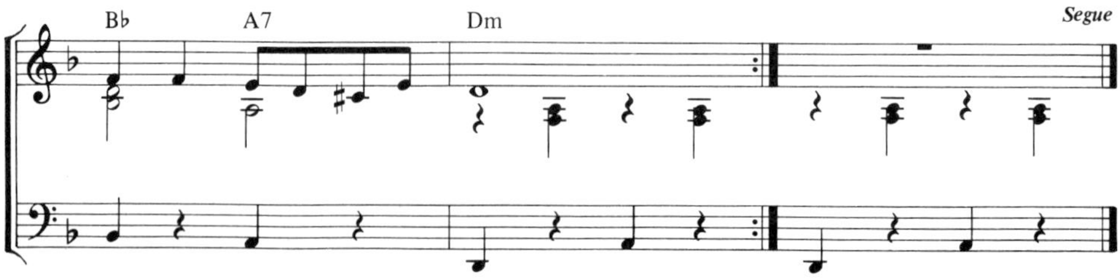

The giving song
(At this time of giving)

Accelerating with each verse

Graham Kendrick

2. May His tender love surround you
At this Christmastime;
May you see His smiling face
That in the darkness shines.

3. But the many gifts He gives
Are all poured out from one;
Come receive the greatest gift,
The gift of God's own Son.

Last two choruses and verses:
Lai, lai, lai . . . *(etc.)*

For God so loved the world

Capo 2 (D)

Graham Kendrick

2. And God showed His love for you,
When He gave His only Son;
And you, if you trust in Him,
Shall not die,
But have eternal life;
No you shall not die,
But have eternal life.

Peace to you

Graham Kendrick

Leader says:
Let's give thanks to God together.

All say:
Thank You, heavenly Father, for the peace that comes through Your gift of Jesus, the Prince of Peace. Thank You that although He was in very nature God, He made Himself as nothing, took on the nature of a servant, was made in human likeness, and experienced the pain and suffering of a sinful world.

Thank You that, in order to give us life, He humbled Himself, and surrendered to death, even death on a cross . . . .

God with us

Graham Kendrick

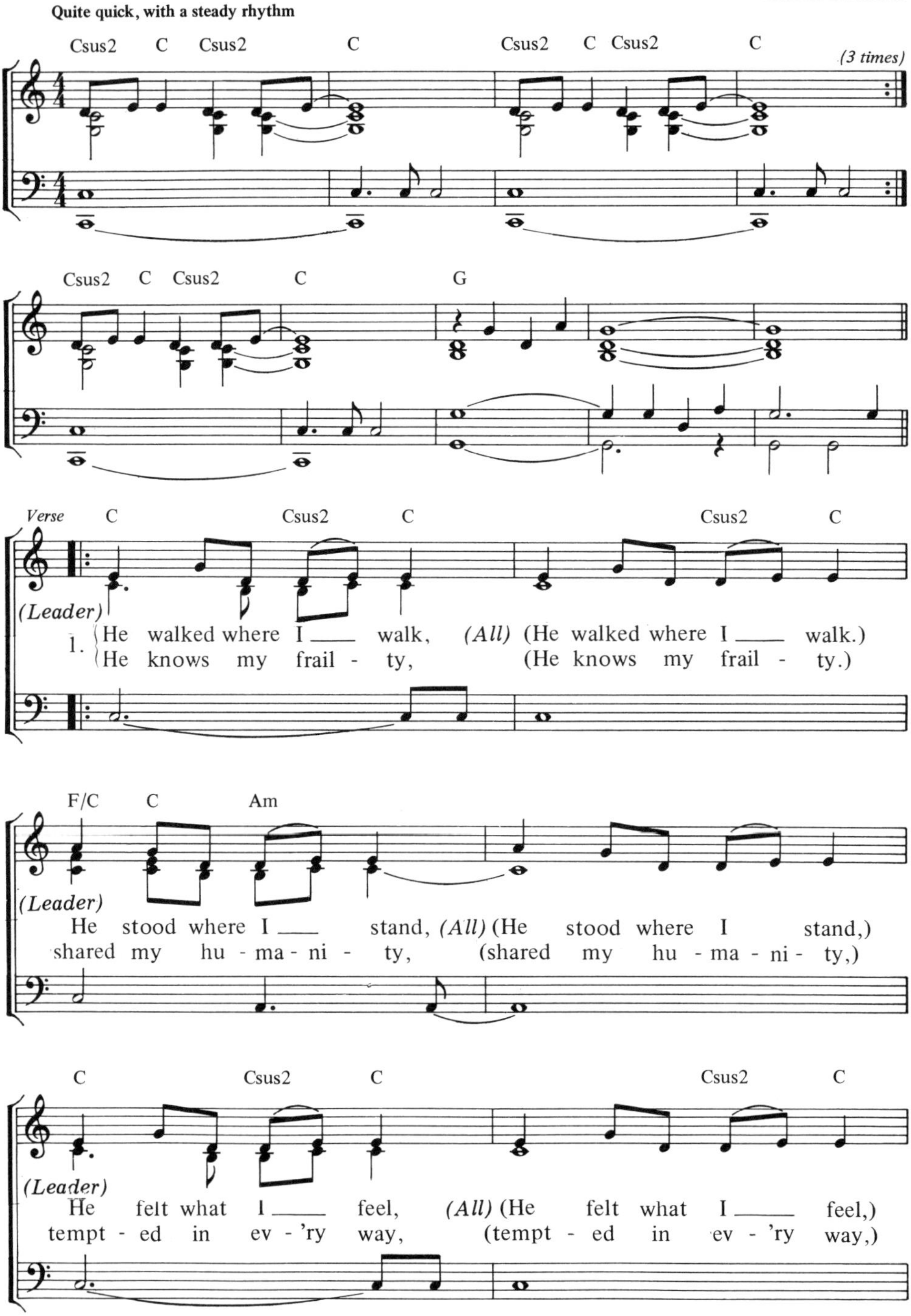

(Leader)	(All)
2. One of a hated race,	(echo)
Stung by the prejudice,	(echo)
Suff'ring injustice,	(echo)
Yet He forgives.	(echo)
Wept for my wasted years,	(echo)
Paid for my wickedness,	(echo)
He died in my place,	(echo)
That I might live.	(echo)

Heaven invites you to a party

Graham Kendrick

2nd time
E
A/E
E
(Leader/echo) And it's for you (and it's for you) and it's for
come'.
door (now hea-ven's door) is o -pen
me, (and it's for me) for all your friends, (for all your friends) and fa - mi -
wide, (is o - pen wide) so come on in (so come on in) come step in -
1st time
2nd time
D.S. al Coda
- ly. (and fa mi - ly.) Now hea-ven's
-side. (come step in - side.)
CODA
E
A/E
come'. An - gels, from the realms of glo - ry,
C♯m
B
E
wing your flight o'er all the earth; you who sang cre -

C♯m
B
E
(Leader/echo) And it's for
a - tion's sto - ry, now pro - claim Mes - si - ah's birth.
you (and it's for you) and it's for me, (and it's for me) for all your
blast, (let trum-pets blast) let mu-sic play, (let mu - sic play) let peo - ple
1st time
friends (for all your friends) and fa - mi - ly. (and fa - mi - ly.) Let trum-pets
shout, (let peo-ple shout) let ban-ners
2nd time
wave. (let ban-ners wave.)
(Leader) Come all you peo - ple, (All) come all you peo - ple,
Send in - vi - ta - tions send in - vi - ta - tions

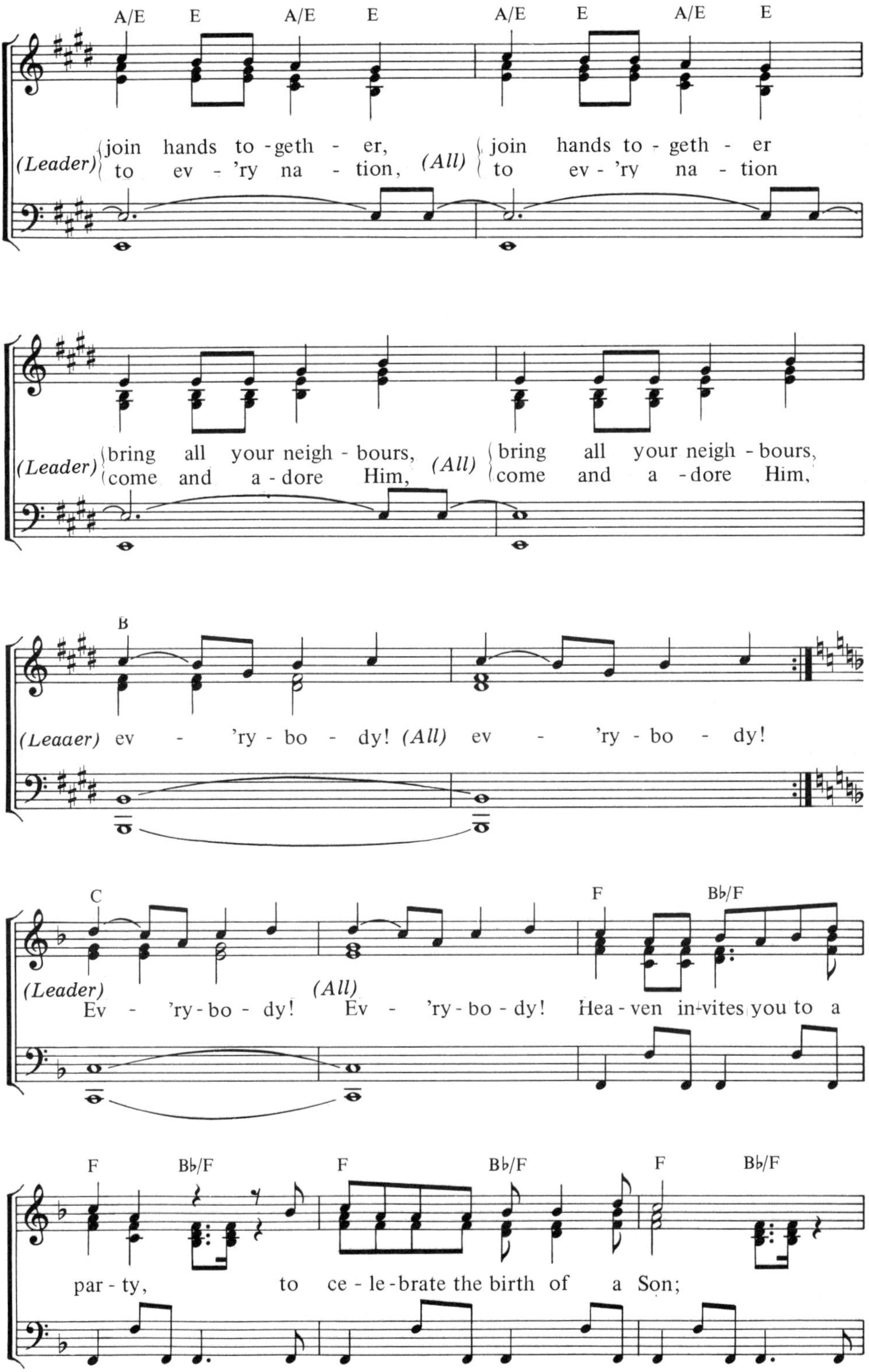
A/E E A/E E A/E E A/E E
(Leader) join hands to - geth - er, (All) join hands to - geth - er
to ev - 'ry na - tion, to ev - 'ry na - tion
(Leader) bring all your neigh - bours, (All) bring all your neigh - bours,
come and a - dore Him, come and a - dore Him,
B
(Leaaer) ev - 'ry - bo - dy! (All) ev - 'ry - bo - dy!
C F B♭/F
(Leader) Ev - 'ry - bo - dy! (All) Ev - 'ry - bo - dy! Hea - ven in - vites you to a
F B♭/F F B♭/F F B♭/F
par - ty, to ce - le - brate the birth of a Son;

F Bb/F F Bb/F
an - gels re - joic - ing in the star - light, sing - ing
F Bb/F F Bb/F
'Christ your Sa - viour has come'. (Leader/echo) And it's for
F
you, (and it's for you) and it's for me, (and it's for me) for all your
blast, (let trum-pets blast) let mu - sic play, (let mu-sic play) let peo - ple
1st time
friends (for all your friends) and fa - mi - ly. (and fa - mi - ly.) Let trum-pets
shout, (let peo-ple shout) let ban-ners
2nd time
Gsus4 G Segue
wave. (let ban-ners wave.)

Tonight (reprise)
(Glory to God)

Graham Kendrick

Thanks be to God (reprise)

Brightly, with strength

Graham Kendrick

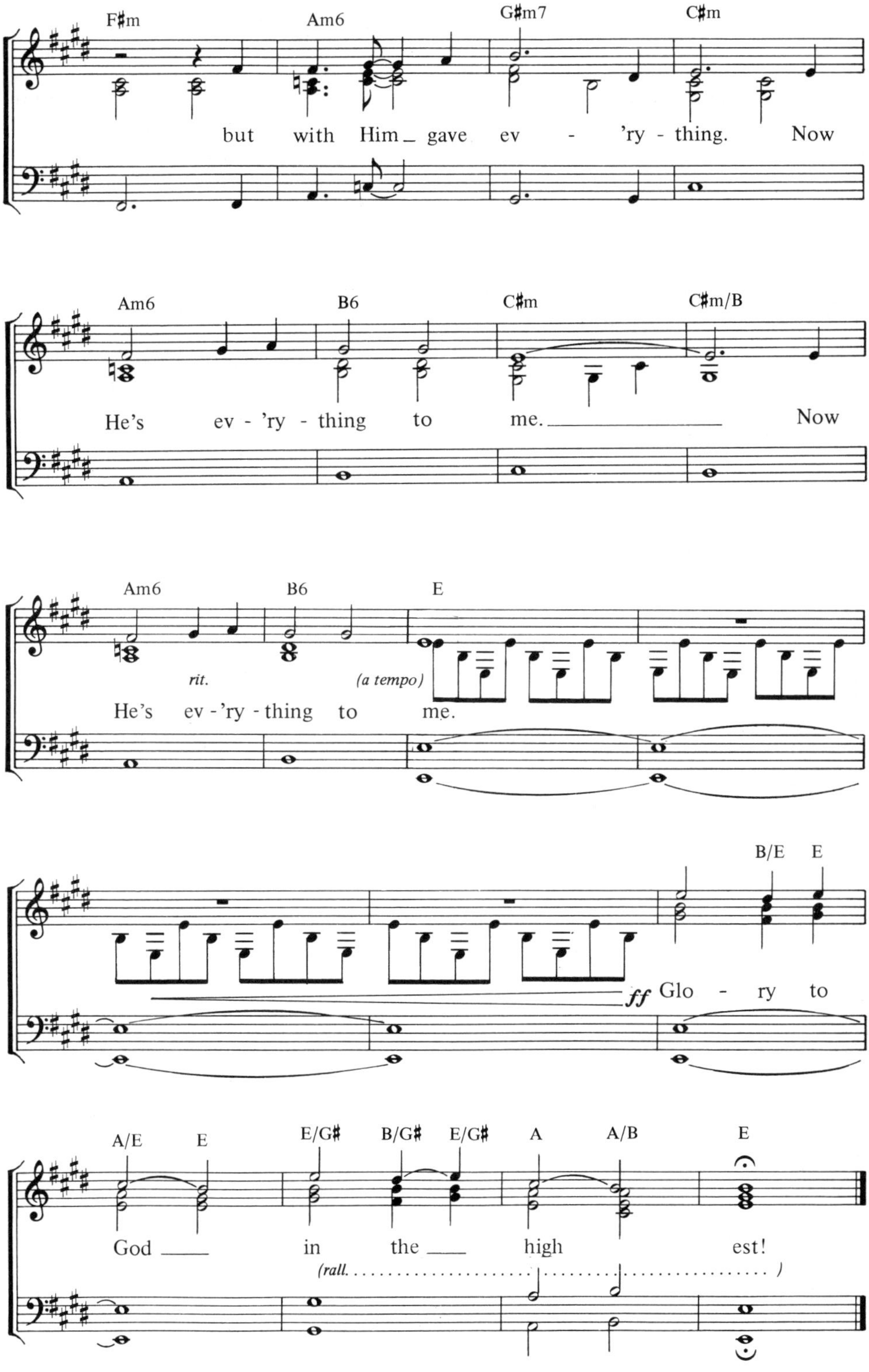
F♯m Am6 G♯m7 C♯m
but with Him gave ev - 'ry - thing. Now
Am6 B6 C♯m C♯m/B
He's ev - 'ry - thing to me. Now
Am6 B6 E
rit.
(a tempo)
He's ev - 'ry - thing to me.
B/E E
ff
Glo - ry to
A/E E E/G♯ B/G♯ E/G♯ A A/B E
God in the high est!
(rall.)

GOOD NEWS

GOOD NEWS, good news to you we bring,
Alleluia!
News of great joy that angels sing,
Alleluia!

Tender mercy He has shown us,
Joy to all the world;
For us God sends His only Son,
Alleluia!

Let earth's dark shadows fly away,
Alleluia!
In Christ has dawned an endless day,
Alleluia!

Now God with us on earth resides,
Alleluia!
And heaven's door is open wide,
Alleluia!

Graham Kendrick.

SING ALL THE EARTH / GLORIA

SING, ALL THE EARTH,
For the Lord,
He has come among us,
Sing all the earth, sing all the earth.
(Repeat, with Women echo)

Come, all ye citizens,
Welcome your God and Creator, *(Men–Women echo)*
Sing all the earth,
sing all the earth. *(All)*

Gloria!
Hosanna in excelsis!
(Repeat)

Graham Kendrick.

'Gloria' words by G. R. Woodward (1848–1934).

ARISE, SHINE

DARKNESS LIKE A SHROUD covers
the earth;
Evil like a cloud covers the people.
But the Lord will rise upon you,
And His glory will appear on you—
Nations will come to your light.

Arise, shine, your light has come,
The glory of the Lord has risen on
you!
Arise, shine, your light has come,
Jesus the Light of the world has
come.
(instead, last time)
Jesus the Light of the world,
Jesus the Light of the world,
Jesus the Light of the world has
come.
Your light has come! (Men)
Your light has come! (Women)
Your light has come! (Men)
Your light has come! (Women)
Your light has come! (All)

Here among us now, Christ the light
Kindles brighter flames in our
trembling hearts!
Living Word, our Lamp, come guide
our feet
As we walk as one in light and peace,
Till justice and truth shine like the
sun.

Leader says:
Welcome to the celebration! Welcome to the greatest birthday party of all time! We are celebrating the birth of a Child whose coming changed the whole course of human history, and who has changed our lives too. Though His arrival was almost unnoticed, His birth had been prophesied centuries before when the prophet Isaiah said:

All say:
For a Child will be born to us, a Son will be given to us; and He will be our ruler. He will be called Wonderful Counsellor, Mighty God, Eternal Father, Prince of Peace.

Leader says:
Let's celebrate together this most joyful of all birthdays, the birthday of Jesus, the Child from heaven.

THIS CHILD

THIS CHILD, secretly comes in the
night,
Oh this Child, hiding a heavenly light,
Oh this Child, coming to us like a
stranger
This heavenly Child.

This Child, heaven come down now
To be with us here,
Heavenly love and mercy appear,
Softly in awe and wonder come
near—
To this heavenly Child.

This Child, rising on us like the sun,
Oh this Child, given to light
everyone,
Oh this Child, guiding our feet on the
pathway
To peace on earth.

This Child, raising the humble and
poor,
Oh this Child, making the proud ones
to fall;
This Child, filling the hungry with
good things,
This heavenly Child.

(Chorus twice to end)

Leader says:
The birth of a child should always be the cause of great rejoicing, but how much more so when the child is none other than God Himself, come to save His people from their sins! So come and join the dance!

O COME AND JOIN THE DANCE

Ldr: O come and join the dance
That all began so long ago,
All: When Christ the Lord was born
in Bethlehem.
Ldr: Through all the years of
darkness
Still the dance goes on and on,
All: O, take my hand and come and
join the song.

Men: *Rejoice!*
Rejoice! } (Women echo)
All: *O lift your voice and sing,*
And open up your heart to
welcome Him.
Men: *Rejoice!*
Rejoice! } (Women echo)
All: *And welcome now your*
King,
For Christ the Lord was born
in Bethlehem.
(Last time only)
For Christ the Lord was born
in Bethlehem,
For Christ the Lord was born
in Bethlehem.

Ldr: Come shed your heavy load
And dance your worries all
away,
All: For Christ the Lord was born in
Bethlehem.
Ldr: He came to break the power of
sin
And turn your night to day,
All: O, take my hand and come and
join the song.

(Chorus, instrumental verse, and chorus)

Ldr: Let laughter ring and angels sing
And joy be all around,
All: For Christ the Lord was born in Bethlehem.
Ldr: And if you seek with all your heart
He surely can be found,
All: O, take my hand and come and join the song.

(Chorus twice to end)

Graham Kendrick.

Leader says:
On that first Christmas night, joyful angels announced peace and goodwill to the world—and heaven is still bursting at the seams with good gifts for everyone. So open your heart to receive what God has stored up for you, especially the greatest gift of all...

THE GIVING SONG

AT THIS TIME OF GIVING,
Gladly now we bring
Gifts of goodness and mercy
from a heavenly King.

Earth could not contain the treasures
Heaven holds for you,
Perfect joy and lasting pleasures,
Love so strong and true.

May His tender love surround you
At this Christmastime;
May you see His smiling face
That in the darkness shines.

But the many gifts He gives
Are all poured out from one;
Come, receive the greatest gift,
The gift of God's own Son.

Lai lai lai lai lai... *(for two choruses and verses)*

Graham Kendrick.

FOR GOD SO LOVED THE WORLD

FOR GOD SO LOVED THE WORLD
That He gave His only Son;
And all who believe on Him
Shall not die,
But have eternal life;
No, they shall not die,
But have eternal life.

And God showed His love for you,
When He gave His only Son;
And you, if you trust in Him,
Shall not die,
But have eternal life.
No, you shall not die
But have eternal life.

Graham Kendrick.

PEACE TO YOU

PEACE TO YOU.
We bless you now in the name of the Lord.
Peace to you.
We bless you now in the name of the Prince of Peace.
Peace to you.

(Repeat 3 times)

(Last time)
Peace to you.
Peace to you.

Graham Kendrick.

Leader says:
Let's give thanks to God together.

All say:
Thank You, heavenly Father, for the peace that comes through Your gift of Jesus, the Prince of Peace. Thank You that although He was in very nature God, He made Himself as nothing, took on the nature of a servant, was made in human likeness, and experienced the pain and suffering of a sinful world.

Thank you that, in order to give us life, He humbled Himself and surrendered to death, even death on a cross...

GOD WITH US

Ldr: He walked where I walk, *(All echo each line)*
He stood where I stand,
He felt what I feel,
He understands.
He knows my frailty,
Shared my humanity,
Tempted in every way,
Yet without sin.

All: *God with us, so close to us.*
God with us, Immanuel!
God with us, so close to us.
God with us, Immanuel!

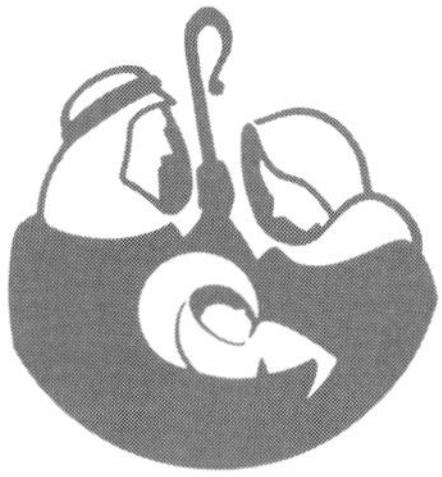

Ldr: One of a hated race, *(All echo each line)*
Stung by the prejudice,
Suff'ring injustice,
Yet He forgives.
Wept for my wasted years,
Paid for my wickedness,
He died in my place,
That I might live.

(All: *Chorus twice to end*)

Graham Kendrick.

HEAVEN INVITES YOU TO A PARTY

HEAVEN INVITES YOU TO A PARTY
To celebrate the birth of a Son;
Angels rejoicing in the starlight,
Singing 'Christ your Saviour has come'.

(Repeat)

(First Chorus)
Ldr: *And it's for you,* (All echo each line)
And it's for me,
For all your friends,
And family.
Now heaven's door
Is open wide,
So come on in,
Come step inside.

(Repeat first verse)

All: Angels from the realms of glory
Wing your flight o'er all the earth;
You who sang creation's story
Now proclaim Messiah's birth.

(Second Chorus)
Ldr: *And it's for you,* (All echo each line)
And it's for me,
For all your friends,
And family.
Let trumpets blast,
Let music play,
Let people shout,
Let banners wave.

Ldr: Come all you people, *(All echo each line)*
Join hands together,
Bring all your neighbours,
Everybody!
Send invitations,
To every nation,
Come and adore Him,
Everybody!
Everybody!

All: Heaven invites you to a party
To celebrate the birth of a Son;
Angels rejoicing in the starlight
Singing 'Christ your Saviour has come'.

(Second Chorus)

Graham Kendrick.

'Angels from the realms of glory' words by J. Montgomery (1771–1854).

TONIGHT (GLORY TO GOD) Reprise

Glory to God
In the highest,
And on the earth
Be peace from heav'n!

(Repeat)

Glory to God
In the highest, } (Men–Women echo)
And on the earth (Men)
Be peace from heav'n! (All)

(Repeat)

THANKS BE TO GOD Reprise

And now thanks be to God
For His gift beyond words,
The Son whom He loved,
No, He did not withold Him,
But with Him gave everything.
Now He's everything to me.
Now He's everything to me.

Glory to God, in the highest!

Graham Kendrick.

'The desire to
relieve the hideous
secularity of our great
towns may well lead to a
demand for the use of carols
in outdoor processions and
festivals in spring and
summer as well as
at Christmas.'

This statement was made way back in 1928 by Percy Dearmer, editor of the *Oxford Book of Carols*. Sixty years later his forecast is being fulfilled. We hope *Make Way for Christmas – The Gift* will help you play your part in taking our 'great towns' (and villages) for Jesus.

Make Way for the Cross

Let the flame burn brighter

CONTENTS

INTRODUCTION

The Cross – symbol of torture, death, injustice, failure and shame – yet becomes the symbol of hope, forgiveness, freedom, justice and mercy to countless millions over twenty centuries.

Make Way for the Cross focuses on the heart of the Christian gospel and carries a strong evangelistic message.

The power of the Cross is on the move as never before through every continent, disregarding borders and sweeping like a forest fire through barriers of race, colour, culture and politics. Ordinary people, especially the poor and oppressed, are discovering that their Creator is also their Saviour. It is time for the whole world to see His glory:

Let the flame burn brighter
In the heart of the darkness
Turning night to glorious day.
Let the song grow louder
As our love grows stronger
Let it shine. . . .

In 1986, *Make Way! – A Carnival of Praise* launched thousands of Christians out onto the streets proclaiming the truth of Scripture in acts of witness, praise and spiritual warfare. *Make Way! – Shine, Jesus, Shine* develops that theme but lays greater emphasis on prayer, particularly intercessory prayer. *Make Way For Christmas – The Gift* is an invitation to everybody to celebrate the birth of God's Son, Jesus Christ, and discover for themselves the 'greatest gift of all'.

For those who have not had previous experience of the 'Make Way' concept, it is important that these notes be read alongside the *Make Way Handbook* (found on pages 5–52) in order to see its wider context and understand the practicalities involved. There are also many useful resource ideas in *Make Way for Christmas* (pages 105–129) which can be adapted for this 'Make Way'.

Make Way for the Cross contains many of the elements of its predecessors, but as its title suggests, it focuses upon the very heart of the gospel. The aim in writing a series of songs that bring to life the historical facts and proclaim the truth and power of the Cross and Resurrection is not only to continue to pray, proclaim and celebrate but to see people turning to Christ in great numbers.

A great revival of Christianity is the only hope for a world in such desperate need: revival born out of prayer and repentance on the part of the church, and the proclamation of the Good News of the kingdom to the people. Central to all this has to be the Cross of Jesus Christ. Jesus said in reference to His approaching death, 'I, when I am lifted up from the earth, will draw all men to myself' (Jn12:32). He does the 'drawing', our mission is to lift Him up.

Graham Kendrick

USING THE SONGS

The varied styles and vivid content of these songs give great scope for a dramatic presentation of *Make Way for the Cross*, either statically or on the move, or both. The possibilities for combining drama, dance, mime and visual aids with the songs are endless and the following is just an outline programme to spark off a few ideas. It involves a vehicle-led procession (provided that the route is suitable) with musicians and some 'core' singers on the mobile stage to help maintain the strength of the music and lyrics, especially during the scene changes. For clarity, songs, shouts, prayers and readings should also be led by someone on the vehicle with suitable amplification. Most of the ideas, however, can be easily adapted for a static situation.

Having a vehicle also gives you the flexibility to put on an evangelistic programme either before or after *Make Way for the Cross*, using it as a stage. You could even make your whole presentation of *Make Way for the Cross* rather like the medieval mystery plays, using the vehicle as the centre stage rather than simply to carry the musicians and singers. How adventurous you are will obviously depend on the amount of resources and creative talent you have available.

Whatever you do, your presentation of *Make Way for the Cross* should bring out the contrasts in the songs; from the solemnity of 'See now here He comes' to the exuberance of 'The feast is ready' and from the serious reality of 'Broken hearts' to the joy and excitement of 'Oh what a morning'.

Make Way for the Cross is going to challenge you, not only in terms of practical organisation, but also in your ability to come up with creative ideas for visual and dramatic interpretation. It demands an understanding of the truth and power of the Cross, and a readiness to apply it to our daily lives. There must be a commitment to follow Christ through death to self and into new life, or the event will lack integrity and have little spiritual power. As local churches we must not only *preach* good news but we must *be* good news to the people around us.

IDEAS AND STARTING POINTS

1 'Lift high the Cross'

To begin the event, the whole crowd sings. Use a dramatic dance to emphasise the fight between light and darkness/God and Satan/ angels and demons. Dress the opposing 'sides' in white and deep red or maroon respectively. Finish with a pronounced silence.

2 'See now here He Comes'

This song introduces the atmosphere of sorrow, as we mourn over our sins that caused such suffering to God's Son. The crowd opens out and 'Jesus', carrying a full-size cross, appears. As the song begins, continue marching with the vehicle in front, 'Jesus' behind the vehicle in a certain amount of space, and the main crowd bringing up the rear of the procession. Note: banners should be lowered at this point so as not to obscure the cross.

3 'Amazing love'

The atmosphere changes to one of heartfelt thanks and worship. If possible, quickly stand the cross up on the vehicle and hide 'Jesus' back in the crowd. During the first verse attach long, 20cm wide red streamers to the horizontal beam of the cross and let them flow over the procession during the second verse: 'And now this love of Christ shall flow like rivers'. Detach at end of song.

4 *Reading*

Face outwards and proclaim the truth to the passers-by. Finish with a big cheer.

5 'Break out with songs of joy'

This is the moment to unfurl 'hidden' flags, banners and streamers, and begin to celebrate the victories achieved through the Cross.

6 'The feast is ready'

Get the celebration atmosphere going with whistles, party poppers, streamers, etc. Some people on the outside of the procession could break off to give out gifts, eg home-made biscuits, party invitations, treats, Easter eggs, daffodils/flowers etc, (see *Make Way for Christmas – The Gift* and adapt its ideas – pages 116 and 118–119). Throw sweets into the crowd from the back of the lorry, keeping on the move. As is suggested for *The Gift* presentation, suitable message tags could be attached to the token gifts.

7 'Broken hearts'

In the main body of the procession, behind the vehicle, form two separate groups: one of ten men, the other of ten women, who sing antiphonally, emphasising phrases such as 'broken hearts' and 'guilty lives' with clear, precise body movements. In a static situation, place the groups in a strategic position such as either side of the area in front of the 'stage'.

8 'Love of Christ come now'

Face outwards to sing the song, calling down the love of Christ on the people. In a static situation speak the benediction strongly while moving to form a circle around the stage.

9 'Come die, come live'

Ensure that the lead voice is featured clearly and strongly.

10 'Oh, what a morning'/'Let every voice be raised'/'Yours be the glory'

Cut loose, celebrating the Resurrection with all you've got! The cross could now be garlanded with flowers, but not in such a way that it looks funereal!

11 'Let the flame burn brighter'

Start passing heart-shaped helium-filled balloons (with a flame pattern on them?) quickly down the procession/crowd until everyone, or at least a good number, has one. Keep hold of them until the last 'now' of 'Let the flame burn brighter *now*', at which point let them go all together – let the flames cover the land! Make sure people know that they should wait for this cue, or the impact will be lost.

Spread the flame, spread the word. Attach a card or leaflet to each balloon, with an address and an invitation to the finder of the balloon to write back telling you where they found it. In return offer them a prize. When the cards come back send them their prize – a New Testament!

When using *Make Way for the Cross* as a procession, try to finish either back at your starting point, or in a suitable place for repeating it statically, putting on an outdoor evangelistic programme or for talking to passers-by, one to one. Further ideas for multiplying smaller street-corner events can be found in the *Make Way Handbook* (pages 49–51).

SUGGESTIONS FOR BANNER SLOGANS

Jesus mends broken lives

For you! (superimposed on picture of cross)

Forgiven!

Come die, come live!

Christ is risen!

Darkness to light

Death to life

Christ has died

Christ is risen

Christ will come again

(The above three could form separate banners carried in sequence)

The price is paid

By His wounds we are healed

The feast is ready!

Quote from Bishop Stephen Neil:

> In the Christian theology of history, the death of Christ is the central point of history, here all the roads of the past converge, hence all the roads of the future diverge.

Quote from John Stott in *The Cross* (*published by* IVP):

> Where is the spirit of adventure, the sense of uncalculating solidarity with the underprivileged? Where are the Christians who are prepared to put service before security, compassion before comfort, hardship before ease? Thousands of pioneer Christian tasks are waiting to be done, which challenge our complacency, and which call for risk.

1 Corinthians 1:18, 27–29:

> For the message of the cross is foolishness to those who are perishing, but to us who are being saved it is the power of God . . . But God chose the foolish things of the world to shame the wise; God chose the weak things of the world to shame the strong. He chose the lowly things of this world and the despised things and the things that are not – to nullify the things that are, so that no-one may boast before him.

Quote from William Booth from the Preface to the original Salvation Army songbook:

> Sing so as to make the world hear. The highest value of our singing after all has not been the mere gladness we have felt because of our salvation, but the joy of pouring out the praises of our God to those who have not known Him, or of arousing them by our singing to new thoughts and a new life.
>
> And sing till your whole soul is lifted up to God, and then sing till you lift up the eyes of those who know not God to Him who is the fountain of all our joy.

Lift high the Cross

Strongly (♩ = 120)

Graham Kendrick

Em Bm7 Em D/F♯ G D/G
(Women) (Men) (Women)
light, dark - ness and light. All heav'n and hell all heav'n and
G Am G D Em D/F♯ F/G
hell (All) bat - tled here.
CODA
C G Am7 F G C G Am7 F F/G
y.
C G Am F G C G
(Leader) (All)
Raise now your voi - ces, give glo - ry and praise Him, raise now Your voi - ces, give
For He has poured out His blood as a ran - som, for He has poured out His
Am F G F G E/G♯ Am
glo - ry and praise Him,
blood as a ran som.
(Leader)
Hell's pow'r is bro - ken, and hea - ven stands op - en,

2. *(Men)* Here once for all
(Women) Here once for all
(Men) Was sacrificed
(Women) Was sacrificed
(Men) The Lamb of God,
(Women) The Lamb of God,
(All) Jesus Christ.

See now here He comes

With feeling (♩ = 120)

Graham Kendrick

2. *(Instrumental, during which is said)*

Leader: Let's say together:

All: "But He was pierced for our sins, He was crushed for our wrongdoing: the punishment that brought us peace was upon Him, and by His wounds we are healed. We all like sheep have gone astray, each of us has turned to his own way, and the Lord has laid on Him the sin of us all."

(Sing) And all they cry is "crucify,"
"Don't want this man for our king."
And all they say, "take him away,"
"His blood shall be on our hands."

Amazing love

Graham Kendrick

Chorus
Am7 Am/G D
maz - ing love, O what sac - ri - fice, the
F A
Son of God giv'n for me. My
Am7 Am/G D
debt He pays, and my death He dies, that
Am7 D
I might live, that
1st time
Am7 G D G/D
I might live.

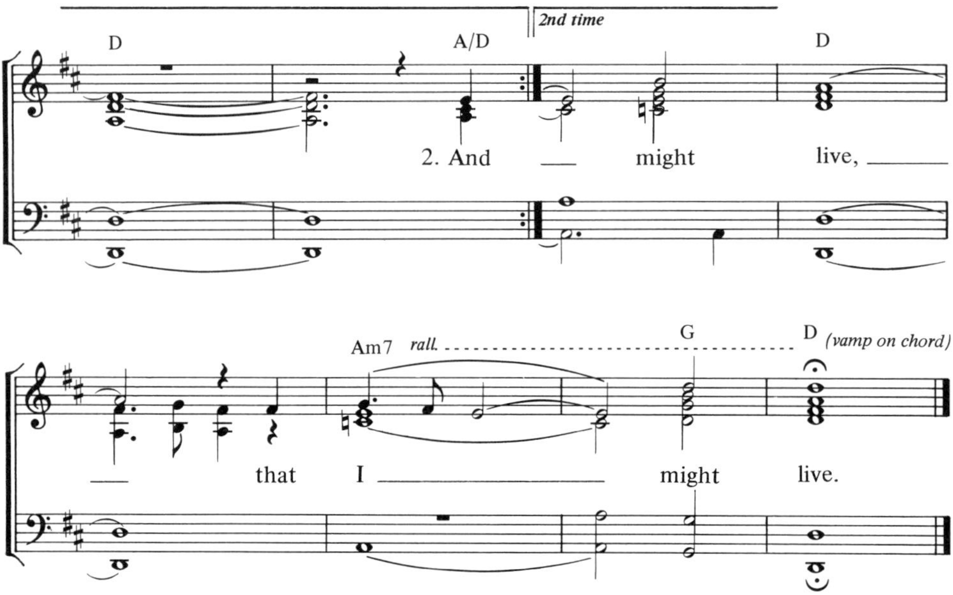

(Optional 1st verse — not for use in march sequence)

(1.) (My Lord, what love is this
That pays so dearly,
That I, the guilty one,
May go free!)

2.(3.) And now this love of Christ
Shall flow like rivers;
Come wash your guilt away,
Live again!

Leader: Let us proclaim together:

All: Christ died for sins once for all, the righteous for the unrighteous, to bring us to God. Therefore God has exalted Him to the highest place, and given Him the Name that is above every name, that at the name of ***Jesus*** every knee should bow, in heaven and on earth and under the earth, and every tongue confess that ***Jesus Christ is Lord***, to the glory of the Father *Amen!*

Break out with songs of joy

(Let flags and banners joyfully wave)

Graham Kendrick

(To be said over introduction)

Leader: We are celebrating today all that Jesus achieved on the cross; how He disarmed the evil powers, cancelled out death, and made the full and final payment for our sins. Let's give Him praise – let's break out with songs of joy!

E/A A F
out with songs of joy. (Women) 3. For
Bb F/Bb Eb/Bb Bb F/Bb Bb
by His cross and by His blood, (All) O praise Him, O
F/Bb Bb F/Bb Eb/Bb Bb
praise Him, (Women) His mer - cy flows, a cleans - ing flood, (All) break
F/Bb Bb G
out with songs of joy. (Men) 3. He
(2nd time slower)
C G/C F/C C G/C C
en - tered hell with a vic - to - ry shout, (All) O praise Him, O

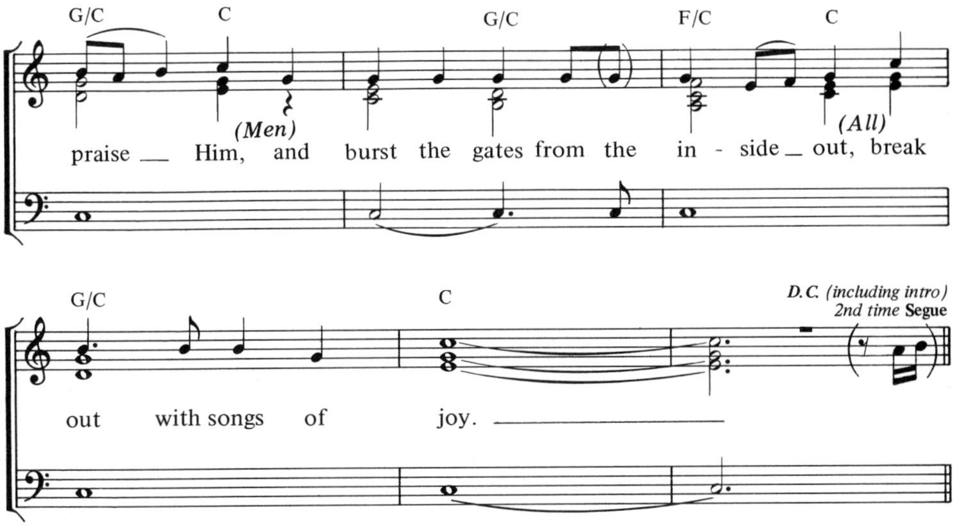

(To be said before verse 4)
(Cheers etc.)

Leader: And having disarmed the powers and authorities, He made an open display of them, defeating them by the cross.

All: Thanks be to God, who gives us the victory through our Lord Jesus Christ!

4. Now death at last has lost its sting,
O praise Him, O praise Him,
And everlasting life begins,
Break out with songs of joy.

5. Now dawns His age of grace and peace,
O praise Him, O praise Him,
When wars shall end, oppression cease,
Break out with songs of joy.

6. Let heaven and earth together sing,
O praise Him, O praise Him,
The glories of our suffering King,
Break out with songs of joy.

(Cheers etc.)

The feast is ready
(The trumpets sound)

In a 'fiesta' style (♩ = 153)

Graham Kendrick

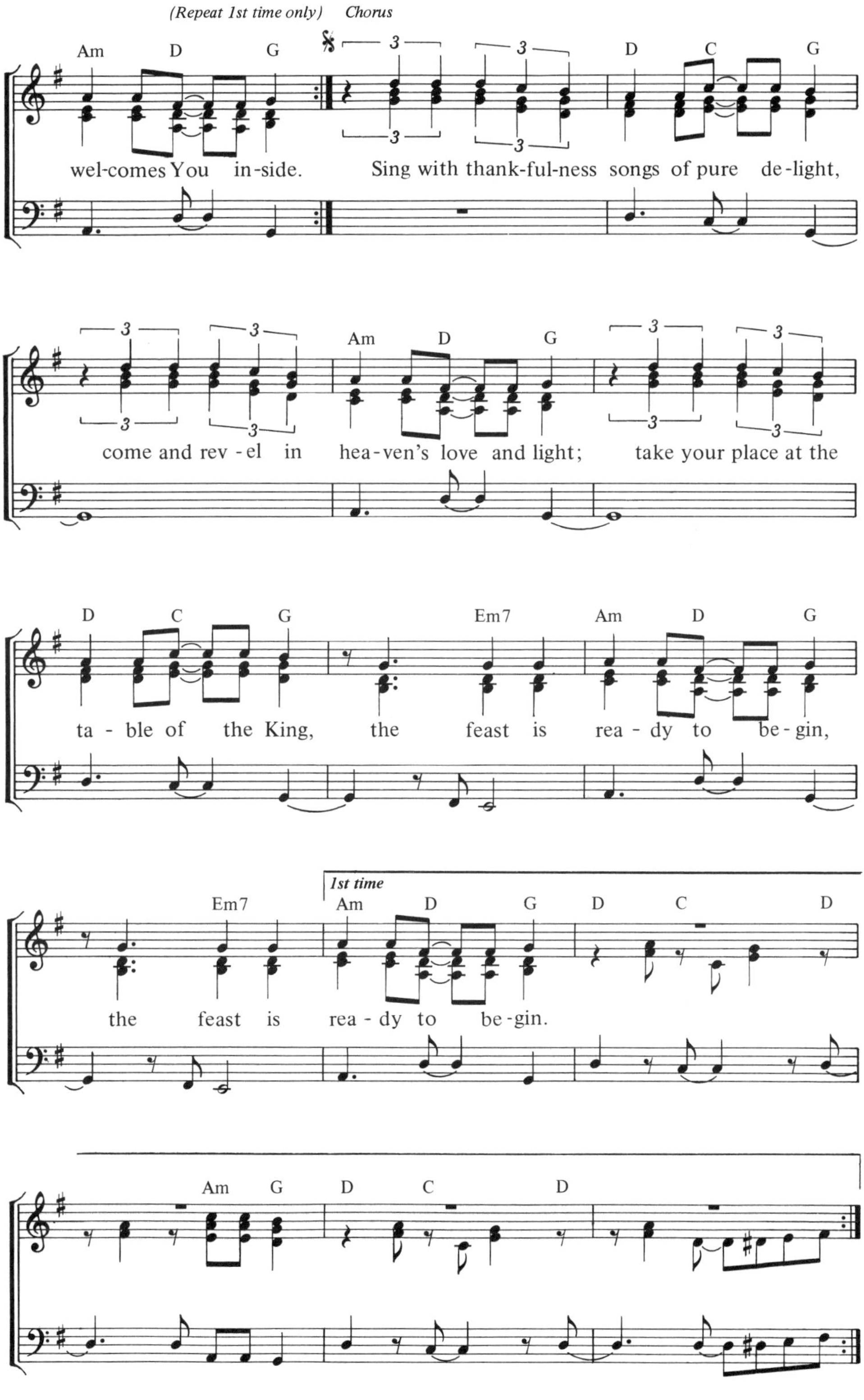
(Repeat 1st time only)
Chorus
Am D G
welcomes You in-side.
Sing with thank-ful-ness songs of pure de-light,
D C G
come and rev-el in heaven's love and light;
Am D G
take your place at the
D C G
ta-ble of the King, the feast is rea-dy to be-gin,
Em7 Am D G
the feast is rea-dy to be-gin.
1st time
Em7 Am D G D C D
Am G D C D

2. Tables are laden with good things,
O taste the peace and joy He brings;
He'll fill you up with love divine,
He'll turn your water into wine.

3. The hungry heart He satisfies,
Offers the poor His paradise;
Now hear all heaven and earth applaud
The amazing goodness of the Lord.

Broken hearts

Graham Kendrick

(To be said over introduction)

Leader: Jesus said:
All: "The Spirit of the Sovereign Lord is on me, because the Lord has anointed me to preach good news to the poor. He has sent me to bind up the broken-hearted, to proclaim freedom for the captives and release from darkness for the prisoners; to proclaim the year of the Lord's favour."

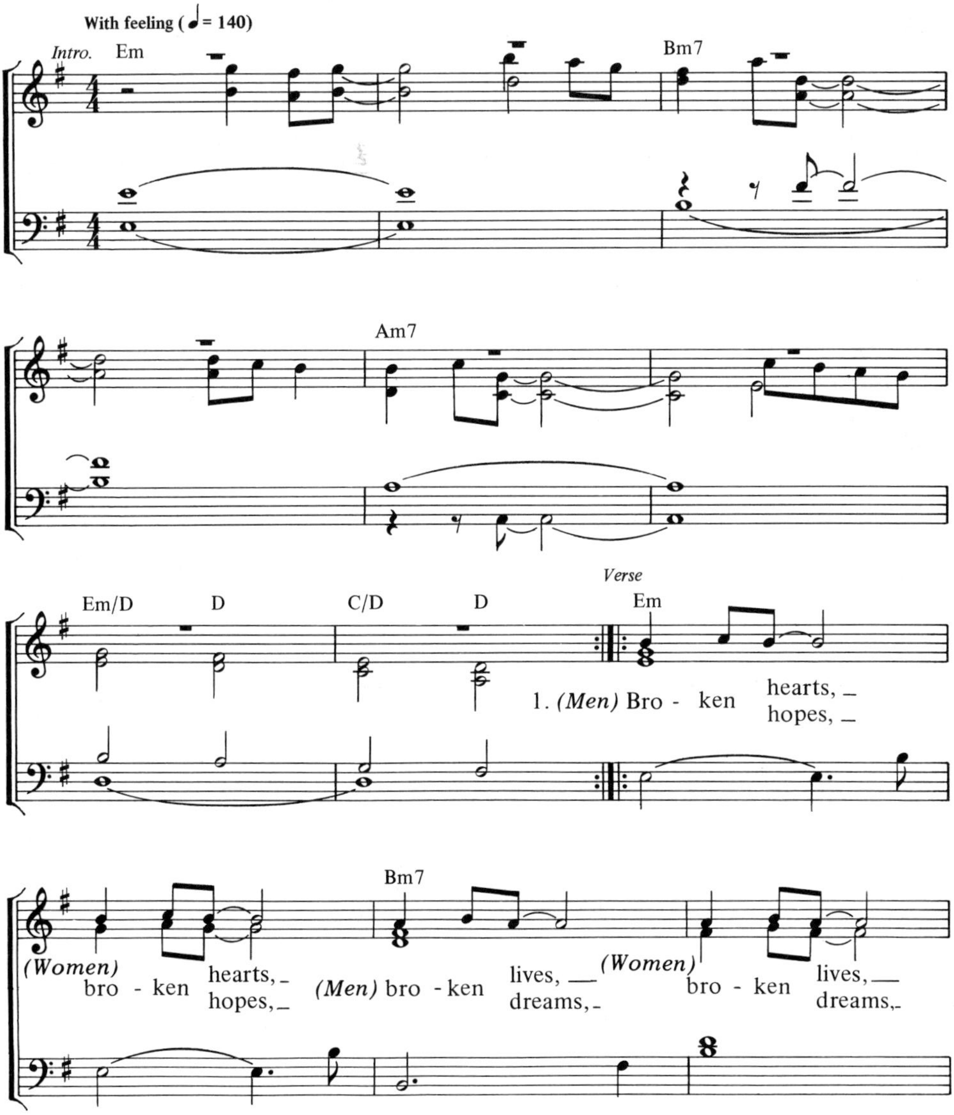

Am7
Em/D
D
(Men)
(Women)
who can mend?
Who can mend?
(All)
Won't you
C/D
D
Chorus
G
D
3
tell me?
Come,
bring them to
Am
Em
D/F♯
G
Je - - sus;
ev - 'ry
D
C
D
1st, 3rd & 5th times
D.S.
G
one,
bring them all to
Him.
2nd time
To next verse
4th time
D.S.
G
G
Him.
Him.

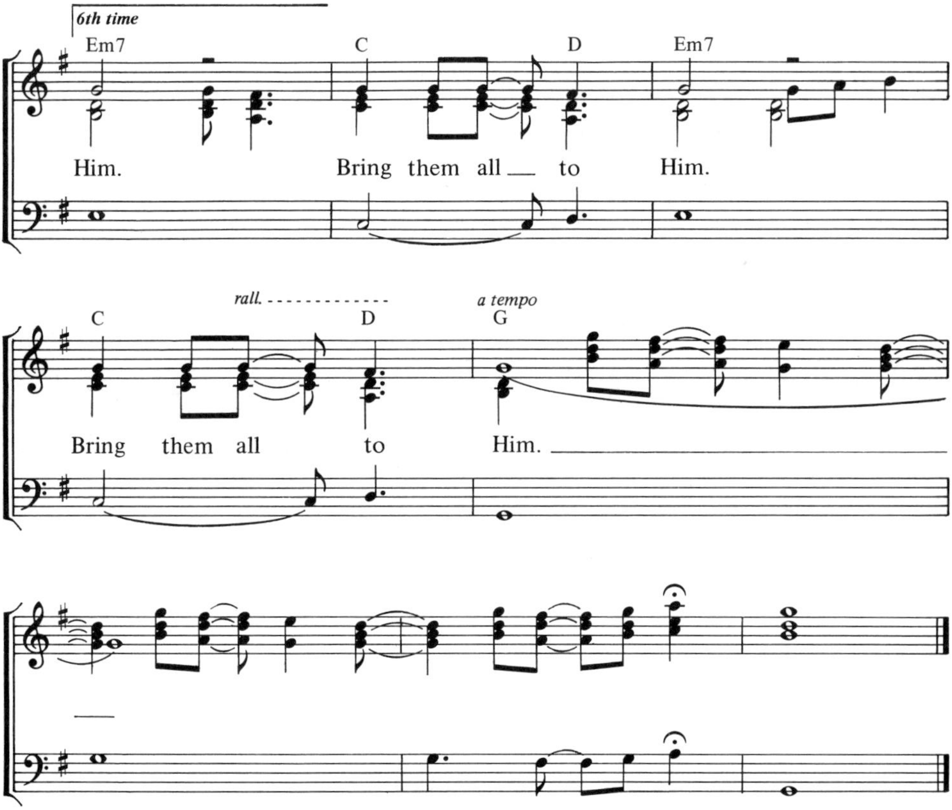

2. *(Women)* Guilty hearts, *(Men)* guilty hearts,
(Women) Guilty lives, *(Men)* guilty lives,
(Women) Who can wash? *(Men)* Who can wash?
(All) Won't you tell me?
(Women) Fearful hearts, *(Men)* fearful hearts,
(Women) Fearful minds, *(Men)* fearful minds,
(Women) Who'll defend? *(Men)* Who'll defend?
(All) Won't you tell me?

Love of Christ, come now

Graham Kendrick

(To be said over introduction)

Leader: Now let's ask God to pour out His love upon all the people around us here.

All: May the Lord bless you and take care of you. May the Lord be kind and gracious to you. May the Lord look on you with favour and give you peace. Love of Christ, come now!

Capo 2 (D)

Steadily (♩ = 116)

G♯m(F♯m)
C♯m(Bm)
G♯m(F♯m)
Flow through here, with mer - cy and
C♯m(Bm) C♯m/B(Bm) F♯m7(Em) A/B(G) B6(A)
grace; love of Christ, come
1st time
E(D) D2(C) F♯m7 (Em) E(D) D(C)
now.
2nd time
E(D) D2(C) E(D)
D.S.
now.
3rd time
E(D) D2(C) F♯m7 E (Em) (D) F♯m7(Em) A/B(G) B6(A)
now. Love of Christ, come
E (D) D2 (C) F♯m E (Em) (D) D2(C) F♯m7 E (Em) (D) D (C)
now.
Segue

Come die, come live
(If any man wants to come after Me)

Graham Kendrick

(To be said over introduction)

Leader: Jesus offers each one of us a new life; but first the old one has to die. He calls us now to lay down our own lives, and to follow Him.

G D G D
(All)
be My dis - ci - ple, if an - y - one wants to be My dis - ci - ple,
C D
(Leader) (All)
let them say 'no' to their own way. Let them say 'no' to their
Chorus
C D Am G/A Am G/A
(Women)
own way. (Men) Come die, come die, come
D C/D D C/D Am G/A
live. come live. (All) This
Am G/A C D
(Women)
is true free - dom. (Men) Come

2. *(Leader)* Whoever fights for the rights to their own life,
(All) Whoever fights for the rights to their own life,
(Leader) Will lose it both now and forever.
(All) Will lose it both now and forever.
(Leader) Whoever lays down their own life for My sake,
(All) Whoever lays down their own life for My sake,
(Leader) Will find it and keep it forever.
(All) Will find it and keep it forever.

Oh, what a morning
(Christ is risen)

Graham Kendrick

(To be said over introduction)

Leader: If we die with Him, we shall also live with Him, for Jesus not only died, He rose from the dead, having broken the power of sin and death once and for all. Let's catch the excitement of those first disciples, as they met the risen Christ, and encountered the explosive power of His resurrection, bringing life which would last forever.

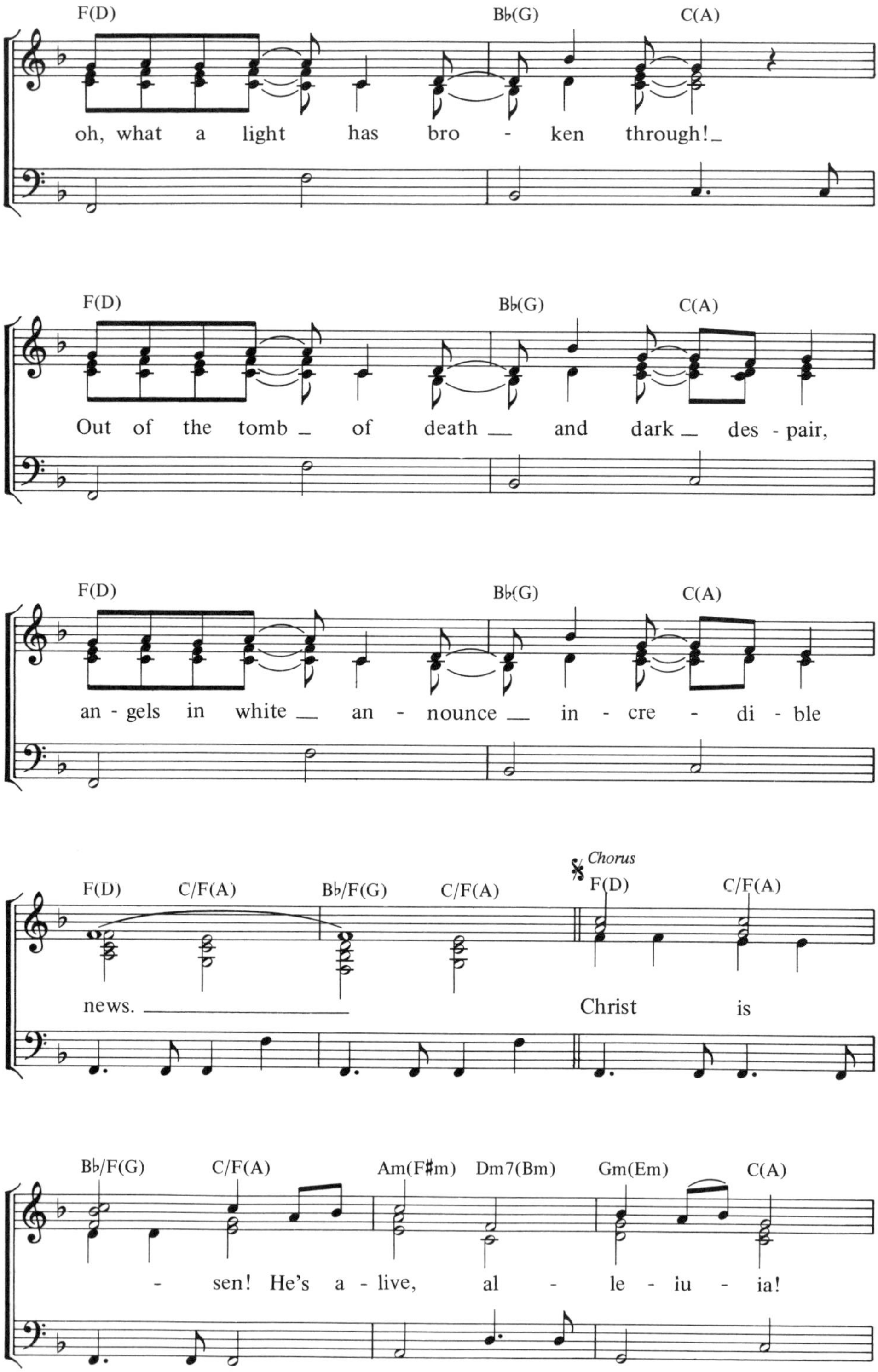
F(D) Bb(G) C(A)
oh, what a light has bro - ken through!
F(D) Bb(G) C(A)
Out of the tomb of death and dark des - pair,
F(D) Bb(G) C(A)
an - gels in white an - nounce in - cre - di - ble
F(D) C/F(A) Bb/F(G) C/F(A)
news.
Chorus
F(D) C/F(A)
Christ is
Bb/F(G) C/F(A) Am(F#m) Dm7(Bm) Gm(Em) C(A)
- sen! He's a - live, al - le - iu - ia!

2. Suddenly hope has filled our darkest night,
Suddenly life has blossomed here;
Suddenly joy has rushed like rivers,
He is alive and love has conquered our fear.

Let every voice be raised
(King of glory)

Capo 3 (D)

Triumphantly

Graham Kendrick

2. The reign of death is done,
All may be free;
Jesus has died and risen
Again in victory.

3. He heals the broken heart,
Sets captives free;
Joy brings to grieving souls,
He shows His love to me.

4. His kingdom shall prevail,
Though nations rage;
This King of love shall rule
And reign from age to age.

Yours be the glory

Music: G.F. Handel
Words: after E.L. Budry (1854-1932)
R.B. Hoybe (1875-1939)

Triumphantly (♩= 142)

Let the flame burn brighter
(reprise)

Graham Kendrick

*The key of this arrangement corresponds to that on the album. However, for street purposes, musicians may find it easier to play this reprise in the key of F, and guitar chords are printed in brackets for this purpose.

1st time
F♯(F) B(B♭) E♭m7(Dm7) C♯(C)
shine! Let the flame burn
2nd time
E♭m7(Dm7) C♯(C) B(B♭) E♭m7(Dm7) C♯(C)
Let it shine! Let it
F♯(F) B(B♭) E♭m7(Dm7) C♯(C)
F♯ (F) G♯m (Gm) F♯/A♯ (F/A) B (B♭) F♯/C♯ (F/C) C♯ (C)
shine! (Men) Let the flame burn bright-er (now.)
(3 times)
F♯ (F) G♯m (Gm) F♯/A♯ (F/A) B (B♭) F♯/C♯ (F/C) C♯ (C)
F♯ (F) G♯m7 (Gm) F♯/A♯ (F/A) B (B♭) F♯/C♯ (F/C) C♯ (C)
now.
(Women) Let the flame burn bright-er (All) Let the flame burn bright-er,
(no chord)
F♯(F)
let the flame burn bright-er now!

LIFT HIGH THE CROSS

LIFT HIGH THE CROSS.
Lift high the cross.
In majesty,
In victory.

Here raged the fight, *(Men–Women echo)*
Darkness and light. *(Men–Women echo)*
All heaven and hell *(Men–Women echo)*
Battled here. *(All)*

Here once for all *(Men–Women echo)*
Was sacrificed *(Men–Women echo)*
The Lamb of God, *(Men–Women echo)*
Jesus Christ. *(All)*

Ldr: Raise now your voices give glory and praise Him, *(All echo)*
For He has poured out His blood as a ransom. *(All echo)*
Hell's power is broken and heaven stands open, *(All echo)*

All: Lift high the cross.

(Chorus to end)

Graham Kendrick.

SEE NOW HERE HE COMES

SEE NOW HERE HE COMES,
Man of sorrows;
Carrying His cross
On to die.

And all they cry is 'crucify',
'Don't want this man for our king'.
And all they say, 'take him away',
'His blood shall be on our hands'.

(Instrumental verse, during which is said:)

Ldr: Let's say together:

All: But He was pierced for our sins, He was crushed for our wrongdoing: the punishment that brought us peace was upon Him, and by His wounds we are healed. We all like sheep have gone astray, each of us has turned to his own way, and the Lord has laid on Him the sin of us all.

(Chorus to end)

Graham Kendrick.

AMAZING LOVE

(Optional 1st verse—not for use in march sequence)

(My Lord, what love is this
That pays so dearly,
That I, the guilty one
May go free!)

AND SO THEY WATCHED HIM DIE,
Despised, rejected;
But oh, the blood He shed
Flowed for me!

Amazing love, O what sacrifice,
The Son of God given for me.
My debt He pays, and my death He dies,
That I might live, that I might live.
(Last time only)
That I might live!

And now, this love of Christ
Shall flow like rivers;
Come wash your guilt away,
Live again!

(Chorus to end)

Graham Kendrick.

Ldr: Let us proclaim together:

All: Christ died for sins once for all, the righteous for the unrighteous, to bring us to God. Therefore God has exalted Him to the highest place, and given Him the Name that is above every name, that at the name of *Jesus* every knee should bow, in heaven and on earth and under the earth, and every tongue confess that *Jesus Christ is Lord,* to the glory of the Father. *Amen!*

BREAK OUT WITH SONGS OF JOY

Leader says over introduction:

We are celebrating today all that Jesus achieved on the cross; how He disarmed the evil powers, cancelled out death, and made the full and final payment for our sins. Let's give Him praise—let's break out with songs of joy!

LET FLAGS AND BANNERS JOYFULLY WAVE,
O praise Him, O praise Him,
In honour of the God who saves:
Break out with songs of joy.

For by His cross and by His blood, *(Women)*
O praise Him, O praise Him, *(All)*
His mercy flows, a cleansing flood: *(Women)*
Break out with songs of joy. *(All)*

He entered hell with a victory
shout, *(Men)*
O praise Him, O praise Him, *(All)*
And burst the gates from the
inside out: *(Men)*
Break out with songs of joy. *(All)*

(Cheers etc.)

Ldr: And having disarmed the powers and authorities, He made an open display of them, defeating them by the cross.

All: Thanks be to God, who gives us the victory through our Lord Jesus Christ!

Now death at last has lost its
sting,
O praise Him, O praise Him,
And everlasting life begins:
Break out with songs of joy.

Now dawns His age of grace and
peace,
O praise Him, O praise Him,
When wars shall end, oppression
cease:
Break out with songs of joy.

Let heaven and earth together
sing,
O praise Him, O praise Him,
The glories of our suffering King:
Break out with songs of joy.

(Cheers etc.)

Graham Kendrick.

THE FEAST IS READY

Leader says over introduction:

In Jesus, God has prepared a feast of good things for all who will accept His invitation. Come on, the feast is ready!

THE TRUMPETS SOUND, the
angels sing,
The feast is ready to begin;
The gates of heaven are open
wide,
And Jesus welcomes you inside.

Tables are laden with good
things,
O taste the peace and joy He
brings;
He'll fill you up with love divine,
He'll turn your water into wine.

Sing with thankfulness songs
of pure delight,
Come and revel in heaven's
love and light;
Take your place at the table of
the King,
The feast is ready to begin,
The feast is ready to begin.

The hungry heart He satisfies,
Offers the poor His paradise;
Now hear all heaven and earth
applaud
The amazing goodness of the
Lord.

(Chorus)

Ldr: Jesus, *(All echo each line)*
We thank You
For Your love,
For Your joy.
Jesus,
We thank You
For the good things
You give to us.

(Chorus twice to end)

Graham Kendrick.

BROKEN HEARTS

Leader says over introduction:

Jesus said:

All: The Spirit of the Sovereign Lord is on me, because the Lord has anointed me to preach good news to the poor. He has sent me to bind up the broken-hearted, to proclaim freedom for the captives and release from darkness for the prisoners; to proclaim the year of the Lord's favour.

BROKEN HEARTS, *(Men–Women echo)*
Broken lives, *(Men–Women echo)*
Who can mend? *(Men–Women echo)*
Won't you tell me? *(All)*
Broken hopes, *(Men–Women echo)*
Broken dreams, *(Men–Women echo)*
Who can mend? *(Men–Women echo)*
Won't you tell me? *(All)*

Come, bring them to Jesus,
Everyone, bring them all to Him.
Come, bring them to Jesus,
Everyone, bring them all to Him.
(Last time only)
Bring them all to Him.
Bring them all to Him.

Guilty hearts, *(Women–Men echo)*
Guilty lives, *(Women–Men echo)*
Who can wash? *(Women–Men echo)*
Won't you tell me? *(All)*
Fearful hearts, *(Women–Men echo)*
Fearful minds, *(Women–Men echo)*
Who'll defend? *(Women–Men echo)*
Won't you tell me? *(All)*

(Chorus twice to end)

Graham Kendrick.

LOVE OF CHRIST COME NOW

Leader says over introduction:

Now let's ask God to pour out His love upon all the people around us here.

All:
May the Lord bless you and take care of you. May the Lord be kind and gracious to you. May the Lord look on you with favour and give you peace. Love of Christ, come now!

LOVE OF CHRIST come now,
Like a mighty ocean.
Flow through here
With mercy and grace.
Love of Christ come now.

(Repeat)

Flow through here
With mercy and grace.
Love of Christ come now.
Love of Christ come now.

Graham Kendrick.

COME DIE, COME LIVE

Leader says over introduction:

Jesus offers each one of us a new life; but first the old one has to die. He calls us now to lay down our own lives, and to follow Him.

Ldr: IF ANYONE WANTS TO COME AFTER ME *(All echo)*
Let them say 'no' to their own way. *(All echo)*
If anyone wants to be My disciple *(All echo)*
Let them say 'no' to their own way. *(All echo)*

Come die, come live;
This is true freedom.
Come die, come live;
Lay down your own life and follow.
Lay down your own life ano follow.
(Last time only)
Lay down your own life and follow.
Lay down your own life and follow.

Ldr: Whoever fights for the rights to their own life, *(All echo)*
Will lose it both now and forever. *(All echo)*
Whoever lays down their own life for My sake, *(All echo)*
Will find it and keep it forever. *(All echo)*

(Chorus to end)

Graham Kendrick.

OH, WHAT A MORNING

Leader says over introduction:

If we die with Him, we shall also live with Him, for Jesus not only died, He rose from the dead, having broken the power of sin and death once and for all. Let's catch the excitement of those first disciples, as they met the risen Christ, and encountered the explosive power of His resurrection, bringing life which would last forever.

OH, WHAT A MORNING, oh how glorious,
Oh what a light has broken through;
Out of the tomb of death and dark despair
Angels in white announce incredible news.

Christ is risen!
He's alive, alleluia!
Yes, He's risen,
He's alive, alleluia!

Suddenly hope has filled our darkest night,
Suddenly life has blossomed here;
Suddenly joy has rushed like rivers,
He is alive and love has conquered our fear.

(Chorus twice to end)

Graham Kendrick.

LET EVERY VOICE BE RAISED

LET EVERY VOICE BE RAISED,
All people sing;
Joining in joyful praise
To Christ, the risen King.

The reign of death is done,
All may be free;
Jesus has died and risen
Again in victory.

King of glory, King of love,
His reign will last forever.
King of mercy, King of peace,
We praise His holy name.
(Last time only)
His name.

He heals the broken heart,
Sets captives free;
Joy brings to grieving souls,
He shows His love to me.

His kingdom shall prevail
Though nations rage;
This King of love shall rule
And reign from age to age.

(Chorus to end)

Graham Kendrick.

YOURS BE THE GLORY

YOURS BE THE GLORY,
Risen conquering Son!
Endless is the victory,
Over death You won!
You won!
Over death You won!

(Cheers etc.)

E. L. Budry/R. B. Hoyle.

LET THE FLAME BURN BRIGHTER
Reprise

LET THE FLAME BURN
BRIGHTER,
In the heart of the darkness,
Turning night to glorious day.
Let the song grow louder
As our love grows stronger;
Let it shine! Let it shine!

(Repeat)

(2nd time)
Let it shine! Let it shine!

Let the flame burn brighter
now, *(Men–Women echo)*
Let the flame burn brighter
now, *(Men–Women echo)*
Let the flame burn brighter
now, *(Men)*
Let the flame burn
brighter, *(Women)*
Let the flame burn brighter, *(All)*
Let the flame burn brighter now!

(Cheers etc.)

Graham Kendrick.

APPENDIX A: Additional shouts to be led by the leader

Here are some further shouts which may be used by the leader.

'ECHO' SHOUTS (*Marchers to echo the leader*)

Some of these are presented as a simple line, some in sets to be used as a sequence. Most of them can be used rhythmically.

Choose life – choose Jesus! (insert love, truth, hope, etc).

Hail – the King of kings!
Jesus – the King of kings!
Let His Kingdom come!
Let His will be done!

The Kingdom is Yours! (or His)
The power is Yours!
The glory is Yours!
Now and for ever!

Glory and honour,
Power and strength,
Wealth and wisdom,
belong to Jesus!

The Lord lives!
The Lord is just!
The Lord is good!
The Lord reigns for ever!

O taste and see that the Lord is good!

Give thanks to the Lord for His love endures for ever!

Great is the Lord and worthy of praise!

Prepare the way of the Lord!

Make way for Jesus!

Hallelujah! For the Lord our God the Almighty reigns!

Christ has died, Christ is risen, Christ will come again!

SPELLING SHOUTS

The leader can shout, 'Give us a "J",' after which all shout, 'J', etc spelling 'JESUS'. He can then ask 'What does it spell?' and other questions with the answer 'JESUS'. Similarly, use words like 'LOVE', 'HOPE', 'PEACE' etc followed by appropriate questions from the leader answered by that word, eg 'What does Jesus bring?' (Leader – write them down and practise beforehand to avoid getting in a muddle!)

CORPORATE DECLARATIONS, PRAYERS AND SCRIPTURES

For corporate reading led by the leader.

1. Yet for us there is but one God, the Father, from whom are all things, and we exist for Him, and there is One Lord, Jesus Christ, through whom are all things, and we exist through Him.

2. We affirm the triumphant power of love. Love that comes from God. Love that was revealed in Christ, God's Son. Love is patient, love is kind, love does not envy or boast. Love is not proud, or rude or self-seeking. Love is not short-tempered and keeps no record of wrongs. Love does not delight in evil, but rejoices with the truth. Love always protects, always trusts, always hopes and does not give up. Love never fails!

3. Love shall finally triumph, and Jesus, the King of love, shall reign forever!

4. O God our Creator, You have made us for Yourself, and our hearts are restless till they find their rest in You.

5. Turn from your sinful ways and be baptised, every one of you, in the name of Jesus Christ, for the forgiveness of your sins. And you will receive the gift of the Holy Spirit!

6. Let the sinner forsake his way and the evil man his thoughts. Let him turn to the Lord, and He will have mercy on him, and to our God for He will freely forgive!

7. Restore us O God, make Your face shine upon us, that we may be saved!

8. In the name of Jesus we stand, by the power of His blood we now claim this ground. Satan has no authority here, powers of darkness must flee, for Christ has the victory!

9. Jesus said: 'I have come that you might have life, and have it in all its fulness'. (Further texts beginning 'Jesus said' may be suitable.)

10. Holy, Holy, Holy is the Lord God, the Almighty, who was, and is, and is to come!

11. All authority, glory and sovereign power belong to You O Lord! All

peoples, nations and men of every language will worship You! Your dominion will be an everlasting dominion, it will not pass away. Your kingdom will not be destroyed– Hallelujah!

12. Now to the King eternal, immortal, invisible, the only God, be honour and glory for ever and ever, amen!

13. You were declared with power to be the Son of God by the resurrection from the dead, according to the Spirit of holiness – Jesus Christ our Lord!

14. 'In the last days,' says the Lord, 'I will pour out My Spirit on all people. Your sons and daughters will prophesy, your old men will dream dreams, your young men will see visions. Even on My servants, both men and women, I will pour out My Spirit in those days.'

15. For God loved the world so much, that He gave His only Son, that whoever believes in Him should not die, but have everlasting life.

APPENDIX B: Guitar chord charts

The following chord diagrams show the fingering for the guitar chords in this songbook.

Key

o = *play open string*	2 = *index finger*	5 = *little finger*
x = *don't play string*	3 = *middle finger*	= *index finger bar*
1 = *thumb*	4 = *ring finger*	**3** = *fret number*

A | B♭ (A♯) | B | C | C♯ (D♭) | D

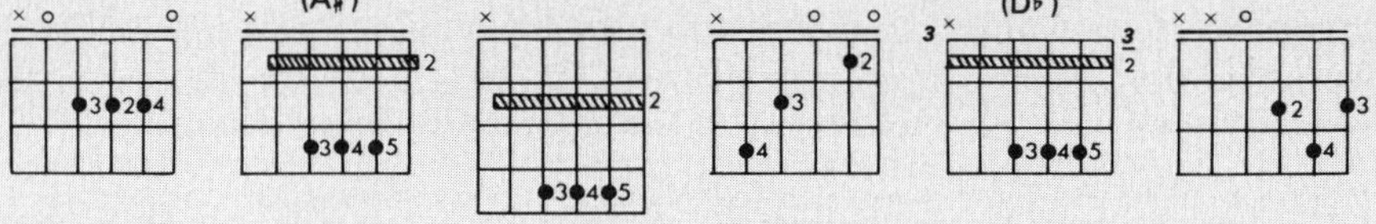

A7 | B♭7 (A♯7) | B7 | C7 | C♯7 (D♭7) | D7

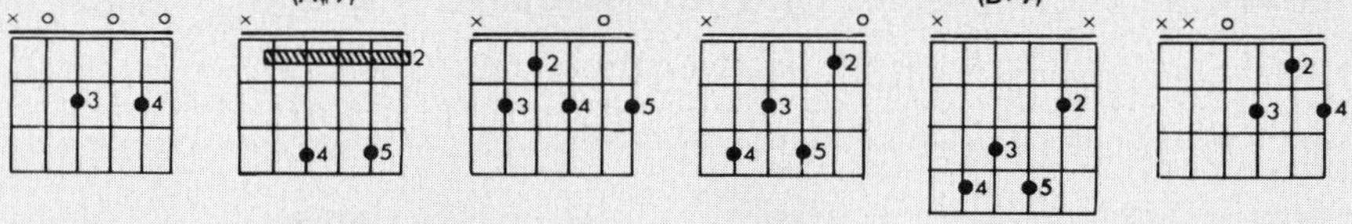

Amaj7 | B♭maj7 (A♯maj7) | Bmaj7 | Cmaj7 | C♯maj7 (D♭maj7) | Dmaj7

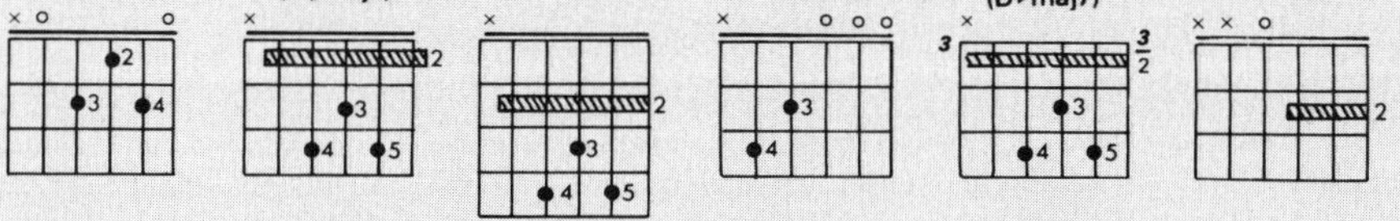

Asus4 | B♭sus4 (A♯sus4) | Bsus4 | Csus4 | C♯sus4 (D♭ sus4) | Dsus4

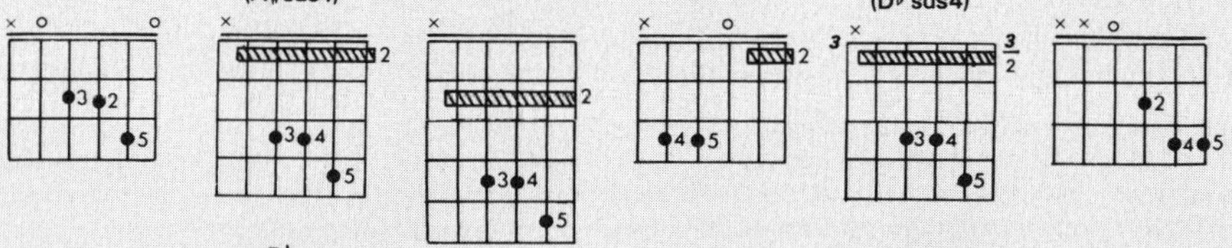

Am | B♭m (A♯m) | Bm | Cm | C♯m (D♭m) | Dm

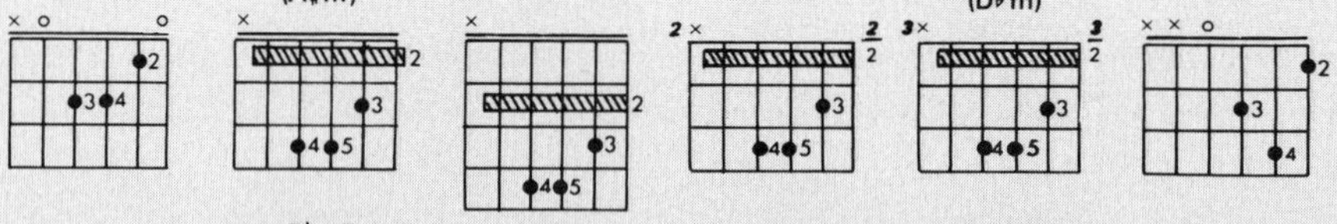

Am7 | B♭m7 (A♯m7) | Bm7 | Cm7 | C♯m7 (D♭m7) | Dm7

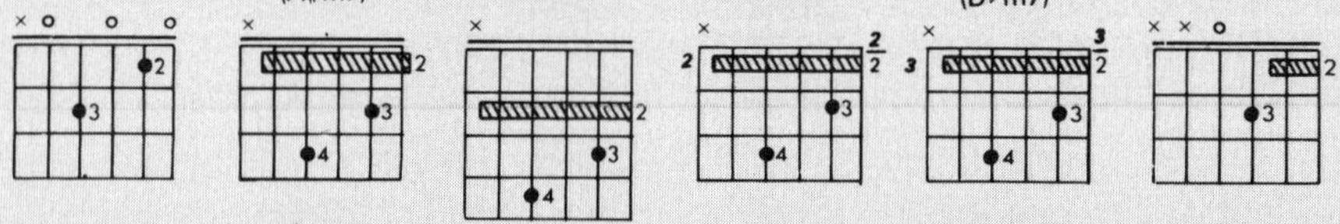

Adim7 | B♭dim7 (A♯ dim 7) | Bdim7 | Cdim7 | C♯dim7 (D♭dim7) | Ddim7

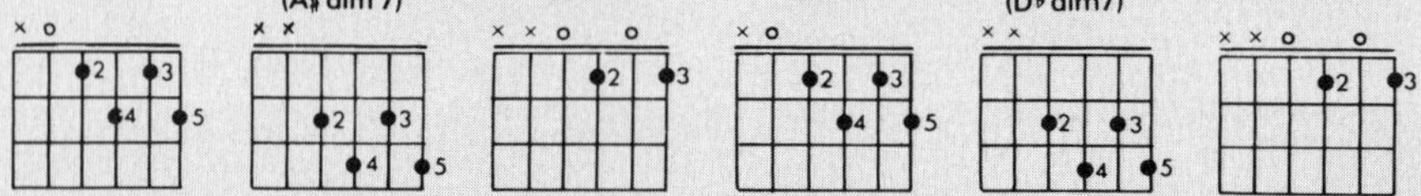

The chords which have been used throughout the book have been carefully chosen with the elementary guitarist in mind. Capo markings, in the left hand corner of many of the songs, allow simple chord shapes to be played with a capo in position. *Capo* 3 (C), for example, means place the capo at the third fret and play the simple chords in brackets, which you will find are in C rather than E . If you use these capo markings you will find that you are able to play almost all of the songs using just ten chords: C, D, Dm, E, Em, F, G, A, Am, B7. If you do see a chord which you don't know, you will probably find that it is playable by mentally stripping it of all its 'extras' e.g. Gmaj7, just play G; Dm9, just play Dm; Csus4, just play C.

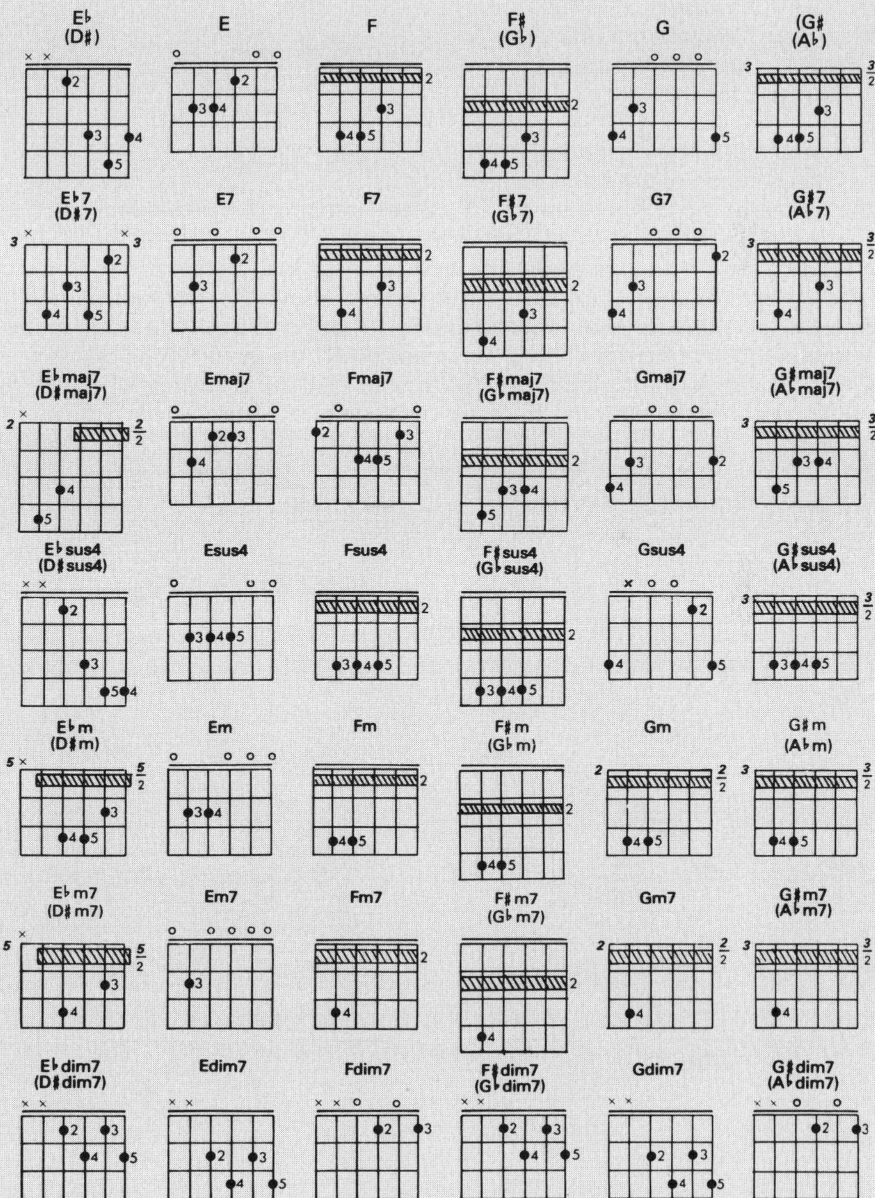

More unusual chords

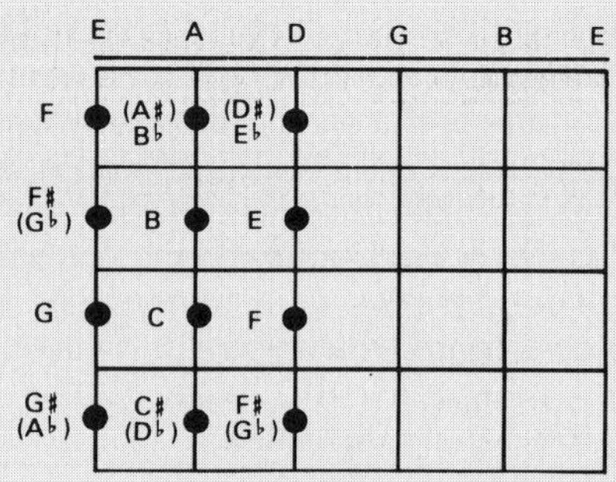

In this songbook you will come across some more unusual chords – mainly chords with different bass notes. If you see D/A, for example, this means play the chord of D with the note A in the bass. For a guitarist who is strumming, this bass note isn't too important and he can just play an ordinary chord of D, but the A bass note is useful for bass and keyboard players, and for guitarists who are picking and want to add colour to their playing.

D/A

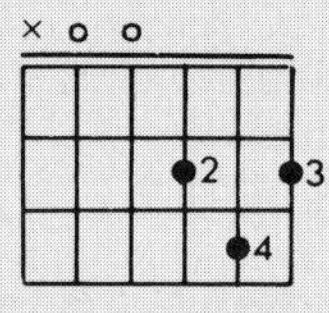

The diagram on the right above shows the position of bass notes on the guitar for those who want to learn them. Looking at the diagram you can work out that a D/A is simple (see second diagram).
As already stated, when *strumming*, the bass note (as long as it is a note from the chord) isn't too important as it doesn't sound above the other guitar strings. Because one requires as loud and full a sound as possible when strumming it is best to play chords which use all six strings. This can be achieved by incorporating a different bass note. Use the following full sounding versions of common chords when strumming. For –

C strum C/G

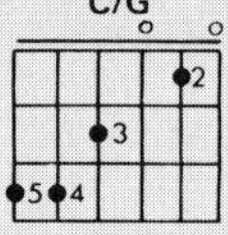

D strum D/F♯

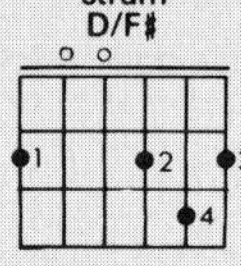

A strum A/E

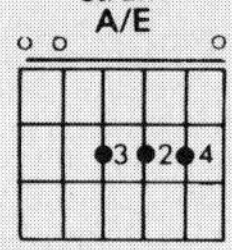

Am strum Am/E

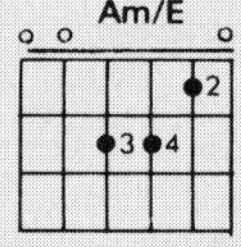

B♭ strum B♭/F

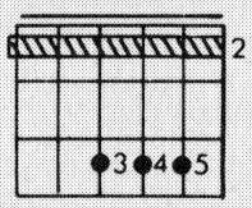

B strum B/F♯

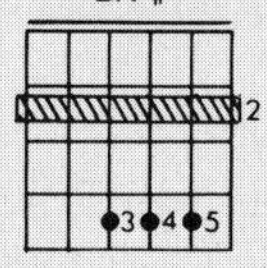

The following are the few more complex chords you will find in the songbook:

Asus²

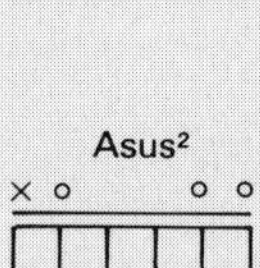

B⁶

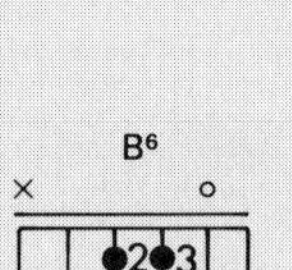

Baug

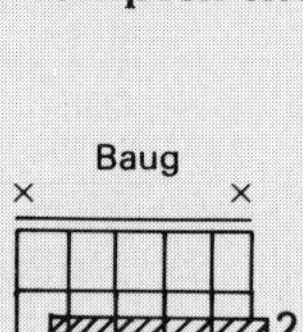

Csus²

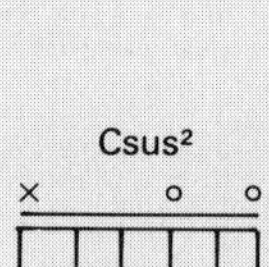

C⁹

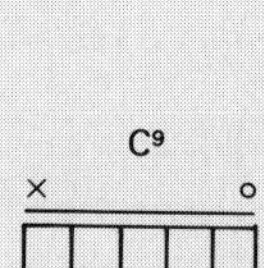

D⁶

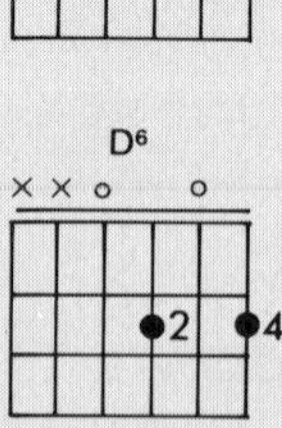

E⁷sus⁴

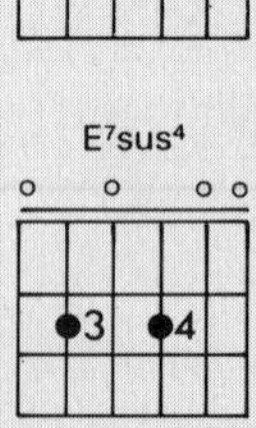

Esus²

Fsus²

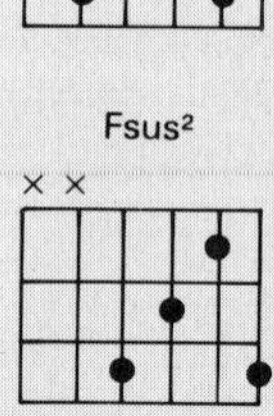

F⁹

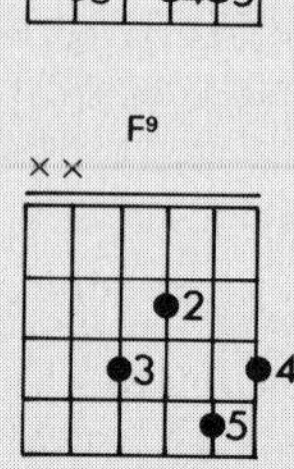

APPENDIX C: Some useful items and addresses

For any information concerning *Make Way*, contact:

Make Way Music Ltd
Glyndley Manor
Stone Cross
Pevensey, East Sussex BN24 5BS
Tel: (0323) 440440

Make Way video and audio ministry tapes on related subjects by Roger Forster. For sale or hire contact:

Ichthus Tape Ministry
116 Perry Vale
Forest Hill, London SE23 2LQ
Tel: 01-669 4208

For details of the Church Copyright Licence, contact:

The Christian Music Association
Glyndley Manor
Stone Cross
Pevensey, East Sussex BN24 5BS
Tel: (0323) 440440

For details of transpositions for brass instruments, and individual instrumental and vocal arrangements for most of the songs in the *Songs of Fellowship* range, contact:

The Songs of Fellowship Arrangement Service
P.O. Box 4, Sheffield
South Yorkshire S1 1DU

Ocarina music and information available from:

Ocarina Workshop
P.O. Box 56
Kettering, Northants NN15 6RH
Tel: (0536) 85963

Your Church and the Media, a workbook by Nigel Sharp. Available from:

Christian Communication
45 Victoria Road
Swindon, Wilts SN1 2AY
Tel: (0793) 34314

Cards and invitations for overprinting available from:

Christian Publicity Organisation
Garcia Estate, Canterbury Road
Worthing, W. Sussex BN13 1BW
Tel: (0903) 64556

What's the Point of Christmas? by J. John. This is a photo-illustrated, quality booklet that is ideal for giving away when carol singing and at Christmas services, as well as for sale in bookshops. The author takes us beyond the traditions, to the baby in the manger and the wonder of God made man. Published by:

Lion Publishing PLC
Sandy Lane West
Littlemore
Oxford OX4 5HG

For details of the Tear Fund leaflet, referred to on p125, contact:

Tear Fund Support Services
100 Church Road
Teddington
Middlesex TW11 8QE
Tel: 01-977 9144

MAKE WAY

INDEX OF TITLES AND FIRST LINES

This index refers to page numbers throughout the book and will enable you to quickly turn-up music or words for any song. First lines where different from titles are shown in *italics*.

MAKE WAY
RESOURCE ORDER FORM

Please fill in the form below (or a photocopy) and then send it, with payment, to
Integrity Music · PO Box 101 · Eastbourne · East Sussex BN21 3UX

Please allow 28 days for delivery.

REF.	DESCRIPTION	PRICE	QUANTITY	TOTAL
MWC1	Make Way for the King (Cass)	£ 7.49		
MWC2	Make Way for Jesus (Cass)	£ 7.49		
MWD2	Make Way for Jesus (CD)	£10.99		
MWT2	Make Way for Jesus (B/Trax)	£ 9.99		
MWC3	Make Way for Christmas (Cass)	£ 7.49		
MWD3	Make Way for Christmas (CD)	£10.99		
MWT3	Make Way for Christmas (B/Trax)	£ 9.99		
MWC4	Make Way for the Cross (Cass)	£ 7.49		
MWD4	Make Way for the Cross (CD)	£10.99		
MWT4	Make Way for the Cross (B/Trax)	£ 9.99		
MWSB1-4	Make Way Public Praise (Combined H/Book)	£ 8.99		
MWC5	Make Way: Crown Him (Cass)	£ 7.49		
MWD5	Make Way: Crown Him (CD)	£10.99		
MWT5	Make Way: Crown Him (B/Trax)	£ 9.99		
MWSB5	Make Way: Crown Him (S/Book)	£ 5.99		
MWV5	Make Way: Crown Him (Video)	£11.99		
			Total cost of materials £	
			Please add 10% for post and packing (20% outside UK) £	
			Total amount enclosed: £	

Name ....
[Please Print]
Address ....

....

....

Postcode ....

Telephone No ....

Please tick method of payment

☐ Cheque/Postal Order enclosed (Payable to 'INTEGRITY MUSIC')

Debit my

☐ VISA ☐ ACCESS/EUROCARD/ MASTERCARD

Card No: ☐☐☐☐☐☐☐☐☐☐☐☐☐☐☐☐

Expiry Date: ☐☐ / ☐☐

Signature ....

PUBLIC PERFORMANCE

Naturally Graham Kendrick is happy for any public presentation of *Make Way* either on the streets, in other open air settings, or in public buildings. You should be aware, though, that these are copyrighted musical works and as such each presentation (other than in the context of a worship service) is subject to the public performance aspect of copyright which is mostly controlled by the Performing Right Society.

Graham's organisation, *Make Way Music*, will gladly take care of any formalities for you free of charge if you send them a completed copy of the form below in advance of the event, together with a stamped, self-addressed envelope. If you prefer, you may send a completed photocopy of this form rather than removing the original from this song book. It will then be available for future occasions.

Although there is no charge for this service, *Make Way Music* would appreciate a contribution to help towards their administration expenses.

DATE OF EVENT ....

BRIEF DESCRIPTION OF EVENT ....

....

IS THE EVENT:- IN THE OPEN AIR – or – INSIDE A BUILDING
(Delete as appropriate)

LOCATION OF EVENT ....

WHICH 'MAKE WAY(S)' WILL YOU BE USING? (please tick)

[ ] **MAKE WAY – A CARNIVAL OF PRAISE**
[ ] **MAKE WAY – SHINE, JESUS, SHINE**
[ ] **MAKE WAY – FOR CHRISTMAS (THE GIFT)**
[ ] **MAKE WAY – CROWN HIM**

ORGANISING GROUP/COMMITTEE ....

ORGANISER'S NAME ....

ADDRESS ....

.... **POSTCODE** ....

TELEPHONE NUMBER ....

APPROX NUMBER OF PEOPLE EXPECTED ....

Please attach a separate list of participating churches/groups. Use a separate form for each event (if more than one). Please send this form together with any contribution (payable to MAKE WAY MUSIC) and a stamped, self-addressed envelope to:

MAKE WAY MUSIC, Glyndley Manor, Stone Cross, Pevensey, East Sussex BN24 5BS.

NOTE: If you are simply performing the songs in a worship service or celebration, there is no need to complete this form.